Charles Barney Cory

The Birds of the Bahama Islands

Containing many birds new to the Islands, and a number of undescribed winter plumages of North American birds. Vol. 1

Charles Barney Cory

The Birds of the Bahama Islands
Containing many birds new to the Islands, and a number of undescribed winter plumages of North American birds. Vol. 1

ISBN/EAN: 9783337257170

Printed in Europe, USA, Canada, Australia, Japan

Cover: Foto ©Andreas Hilbeck / pixelio.de

More available books at **www.hansebooks.com**

THE BIRDS

OF THE

BAHAMA ISLANDS

CONTAINING

Many birds new to the Islands, and a number of undescribed
winter plumages of North American birds.

By CHARLES B. CORY,

CURATOR OF BIRDS IN THE BOSTON SOCIETY OF NATURAL HISTORY, FELLOW OF THE LINNEAN AND
ZOOLOGICAL SOCIETIES OF LONDON, MEMBER OF THE AMERICAN ORNITHOLOGISTS' UNION, OF
THE BRITISH ORNITHOLOGISTS' UNION, OF THE SOCIÉTÉ ZOOLOGIQUE DE FRANCE, ETC.
HONORARY MEMBER OF THE CALIFORNIA ACADEMY OF SCIENCES, CORRE-
SPONDING MEMBER OF THE NEW YORK ACADEMY OF SCIENCES, OF
THE CHICAGO ACADEMY OF SCIENCES, ETC., ETC.

AUTHOR OF

*The Beautiful and Curious Birds of the World, The Birds of the Bahama
Islands, The Birds of Haiti and San Domingo, A Naturalist in the
Magdalen Islands, A List of the Birds of the West Indies,
The Birds of the West Indies, etc., etc., etc.*

REVISED EDITION.

ESTES & LAURIAT.
BOSTON, U. S. A.
1890.

CHARLES B. CORY

PREFACE TO REVISED EDITION.

During the ten years which have passed since the publication of the "Birds of the Bahama Islands" so much has been added to our knowledge of the natural history of the islands, and so many changes have been made in the nomenclature of the subject, that it has been thought advisable to issue the few remaining copies of the first edition in the form of a revised edition, giving the species or races described or eliminated, and whatever changes that have been made during that time.

Although much has been learned regarding the natural history of the West Indies, during the past ten years, a great deal yet remains to be done, especially in the interior of some of the larger islands. It is probable that Great Bahama, Abaco, Maraguana, Inagua, and in fact, many of the islands, still contain much which would well repay the naturalist who would take the time and trouble to properly explore them.

C. B. C.

PREFACE.

The Bahama Islands have, of late years, become such a popular resort, and so many people visit them every winter for the enjoyment of the *dolce far niente* life and magnificent climate always found in those semi-tropical regions, that I have been induced to publish the present volume, with the hope of being able to throw some light upon a subject in which most travellers, as well as scientists, are interested, viz., the many species of birds which are resident or occasional visitants to those islands, about which, at present, so very little is known. I shall commence with a short account of my personal experiences while cruising among the islands, in order to give some idea of the nature and customs of the country, and the best localities for the ornithologist and sportsman to visit.

Part II. will be devoted to ornithology, giving a list of the species found on the islands, with notes regarding their habits, migrations, etc.

In the descriptions of the birds, I have endeavored to point out the characters by which allied species may most easily be distinguished from one another, and in species which resemble each other so much as to render identification difficult, the characteristic points of difference are put in italics.

In conclusion, I wish to express my sincere thanks to my ornithological friends in general, for their kind assistance, and especially to Mr. GEORGE N. LAWRENCE, of New York, for much valuable information.

C. B. CORY.

CONTENTS.

PART I.

	PAGE
PREFACE	3
THE BAHAMA ISLANDS	11
NASSAU	16
THE EXUMA KEYS	21
ANDROS ISLAND	24
LONG ISLAND	26
THE MIRAPORVOS	32
INAGUA	35
MEASUREMENT OF SPECIMENS	39
WORKS AND PAPERS REFERRED TO	40
ABBREVIATIONS OF AUTHORS' NAMES	41

PART II.

BIRDS OF THE BAHAMA ISLANDS		43
FAMILY TURDIDÆ	THRUSHES	45
FAMILY SYLVIIDÆ		52

CONTENTS.

		PAGE
FAMILY SYLVICOLIDÆ	WARBLERS	54
FAMILY CŒREBIDÆ .	CREEPERS	76
FAMILY HIRUNDINIDÆ	SWALLOWS	78
FAMILY VIREONIDÆ .	VIREOS .	82
FAMILY FRINGILLIDÆ	FINCHES .	85
FAMILY ICTERIDÆ	STARLINGS	97
FAMILY TYRANNIDÆ	FLYCATCHERS .	99
FAMILY CAPRIMULGIDÆ .	GOATSUCKERS .	104
FAMILY TROCHILIDÆ	HUMMING BIRDS	108
FAMILY ALCEDINIDÆ	KINGFISHERS .	115
FAMILY CUCULIDÆ	CUCKOOS	116
FAMILY PICIDÆ	WOODPECKERS	120
FAMILY PSITTACIDÆ .	PARROTS	123
FAMILY STRIGIDÆ	OWLS	125
FAMILY FALCONIDÆ .	FALCONS	128
FAMILY CATHARTIDÆ	VULTURES	134
FAMILY COLUMBIDÆ	PIGEONS .	137
FAMILY PERDICIDÆ	PARTRIDGES	142
FAMILY CHARADRIIDÆ	PLOVERS .	144
FAMILY HÆMATOPODIDÆ	OYSTER CATCHERS .	150
FAMILY RECURVIROSTRIDÆ .	STILTS	153

CONTENTS.

		PAGE
FAMILY SCOLOPACIDÆ	SNIPES	156
FAMILY TANTALIDÆ	SPOONBILLS	164
FAMILY ARDEIDÆ	HERONS	166
FAMILY RALLIDÆ	RAILS	176
FAMILY PHŒNICOPTERIDÆ	FLAMINGOES	180
FAMILY ANATIDÆ	DUCKS	182
FAMILY SULIDÆ	GANNETS	191
FAMILY PELECANIDÆ	PELICANS	196
FAMILY GRACULIDÆ	CORMORANTS	198
FAMILY TACHYPETIDÆ	MAN-OF-WAR, ETC.	200
FAMILY PHAETHONTIDÆ	TROPIC BIRD	204
FAMILY LARIDÆ	GULLS, TERNS	208
FAMILY PROCELLARIIDÆ	PETRELS	218
FAMILY PODICIPIDÆ	GREBES	222
DISTRIBUTION OF SPECIES		225

APPENDIX	233
INDEX	241

INDEX OF PLATES.

CROTOPHAGA ANI	ANI .	FRONTISPIECE.
MIMOCICHLA PLUMBEA	PLUMBEOUS THRUSH .	45
SPINDALIS ZENA	BAHAMA FINCH .	92
SAUROTHERA BAHAMENSIS .	BAHAMA CUCKOO	116
ARDEA CYANIROSTRIS	INAGUA HERON .	168
PHŒNICOPTERUS RUBER	FLAMINGO .	180
DAFILA BAHAMENSIS	BAHAMA DUCK .	185
STERNA ANOSTILETA	BRIDLED TERN .	215

ORNITHOLOGICAL BIBLIOGRAPHY

OF THE

BAHAMA ISLANDS.

The Natural History of Carolina, Florida, and the Bahama Islands. 2 vols. Illustrated. By Mark Catesby. London : 1754.

A List of the Birds seen at the Bahamas from Jan. 20 to May 14, 1859, with Descriptions of new or little known Species. By Dr. H. Bryant. Proc. Boston Soc. Nat. Hist., VII., p. 102, 1859. Boston : 1859.

Descriptions of two Birds from the Bahama Islands, hitherto undescribed. By Dr. H. Bryant. Proc. Boston Soc. Nat. Hist., IX., p. 279, 1864. Boston : 1864.

Remarks on the Genus Galeoscoptes, Cabanis, with the Characters of two new Genera, and a Description of *Turdus plumbeous*, Linn. By Dr. H. Bryant. Proc. Boston Soc. Nat. Hist., IX., p. 369, 1865. Boston : 1865.

Additions to a List of Birds seen at the Bahamas. By Dr. H. Bryant. Proc. Boston Soc. Nat. Hist., XI., p. 63, 1866. Boston : 1866.

The Humming Birds of the West Indies. By D. G. Elliot. Ibis, p. 345, 1872. London : 1872.

List of Birds, chiefly Visitors from North America, seen and killed in the Bahamas in July, August, October, November, and December, 1876. By N. B. Moore. Proc. Boston Soc. Nat. Hist., XIX., p. 241, 1877. Boston : 1877.

ORNITHOLOGICAL BIBLIOGRAPHY.

Notes of a few Birds, observed at New Providence, Bahama Islands; not included in Dr. Bryant's List of 1859. By L. J. K. Brace. Proc. Boston Soc. Nat. Hist., XIX., p. 240. 1877.　　　　　　　　　　　　　　　　　　　　　　Boston: 1877.

Observations on some Birds seen near Nassau, New Providence, in the Bahama Islands. By N. B. Moore. Proc. Boston Soc. Nat. Hist., XIX., p. 243, 1877.
　　　　　　　　　　　　　　　　　　　　　　　　　　　　　　Boston: 1877.

The Birds of the Bahama Islands. 1 vol. Illustrated. By Charles B. Cory.
　　　　　　　　　　　　　　　　　　　　　　　　　　　　　　Boston: 1880.

Description of four new Species of Birds from the Bahama Islands. By R. Ridgway. Auk, III., p. 334, 1886.　　　　　　　　　　　　　　　　　New York: 1886.

Five new Species of Birds from the Bahamas. By C. J. Maynard. The American Exchange and Mart, Vol. III., No. 6, p. 69, Feb. 5, 1887.　　　Boston: 1887.

Description of supposed new Birds from Lower California, Sonora, and Chihuahua, Mexico, and the Bahamas. By William Brewster. Auk, V., p. 82, 1888.
　　　　　　　　　　　　　　　　　　　　　　　　　　　　　　New York: 1888.

The Birds of the West Indies, including all Species known to occur in the Bahama Islands, the Greater Antilles, the Caymans, and the Lesser Antilles, excepting the Islands of Tobago and Trinidad. Auk, Vol. III., pp. 1, 187, 337, 454 (1866); Vol. IV., pp. 37, 108, 223, 311 (1887); and Vol. V., pp. 48, 155 (1888); also revised in book form, with maps and added illustrations. 1 vol. By Charles B. Cory.
　　　　　　　　　　　　　　　　　　　　　　　　　　　　　　Boston: 1889.

Description of a new Species of Icterus from Andros Island, Bahamas. By J. A. Allen. Auk, VII., p. 343, 1890.　　　　　　　　　　　　　　　New York: 1890.

The Birds of the Bahama Islands. Revised edition. 1 vol. Illustrated. By C. B. Cory.
　　　　　　　　　　　　　　　　　　　　　　　　　　　　　　Boston: 1890.

SPECIES AND SUBSPECIES DESCRIBED SINCE 1880.

POLIOPTILA CÆRULEA CÆSIOGASTER. Ridgw.

BAHAMA GNAT-CATCHER.

Polioptila cærulea cæsiogaster. Ridgway, Manual N. A. Birds, p. 569 (1887); Cory, Birds of the West Indies, p. 37 (1889).

SP. CHAR. — " Lower parts light bluish gray, deeper laterally; upper parts deep bluish plumbeous, somewhat bluer on top of the head, but scarcely, if any at all, paler on rump. About the size of *P. cærulea.*" — *Ridgw., l. c.*

HABITAT. Bahama Islands. (Resident.)

GEOTHLYPIS CORYI. Ridgw.

CORY'S YELLOW-THROATED WARBLER.

Geothlypis coryi. Ridgw., Auk, III., pp. 334, 335 (1886); Cory, Birds of the West Indies, p. 287 (1889).

SP. CHAR. — " In plumage much resembling *G. beldingi nobis* (from Lower California), but yellow of lower parts with less of an orange tint, the sides and upper parts without any olive-brown tinge; the flanks bright greenish yellow, and the yellow posterior border to the black 'mask' much narrower and less purely yellow. Form very different; the bill about twice as large, and of different shape. Female very different from that of any other known species, being bright olive-green above and entirely pure gamboge yellow below, with ashy auriculars and yellowish forehead, and superciliary stripe. Black mask bordered by yellow, and not ashy, as in *G. rostratus.*" — *Ridgway, orig. descr. l. c.*

HABITAT. Eleuthera Island.

GEOTHLYPIS TANNERI. Ridgw.

TANNER'S YELLOW-THROATED WARBLER.

Geothlypis tanneri. Ridgway, Auk, III., p. 335 (1886); Cory, Birds of the West Indies, p. 287 (1889).

Described as "similar to *G. coryi,* but bill more robust and straighter, black of the forehead more extended, yellow posterior border to 'mask' paler, and changing to yellowish gray across crown; olive-green of upper parts much duller, and yellow of lower parts less intense."

HABITAT. Abaco Island, Bahamas.

GEOTHLYPIS TRICHAS RESTRICTUS. (Maynard.)

Geothlypis restricta. Maynard, American Exchange and Mart, p. 69, Feb. 5, 1887.

A somewhat doubtful resident subspecies, which may prove to be a fairly well marked race. It is described as differing from

G. *trichas* in having the black mask restricted on the cheeks to the same width as on the forehead, with the space next to the black abruptly ashy, and the wings shorter and rounder.

Bahamas.

VIREO ALLENI. Cory.

ALLEN'S VIREO.

Vireo alleni. Cory, Auk, III., pp. 500, 501 (1886); *Ib.*, Birds of the West Indies, p. 75 (1889).

Vireo crassirostris flavescens. Ridgw., Manual N. A. Birds, p. 476 (1887).

Sp. Char. — Above dull olive, showing a dull yellow tinge on the forehead; a stripe of yellow from the upper mandible to the eye, the yellow showing on the upper and lower eyelids; entire under surface dull yellow, tinged with olive on the flanks and sides; two distinct, yellowish white wing bands; quills dark brown, most of the feathers edged with yellowish green on the outer webs; tail brown, showing faint olive edgings on the outer webs; bill horn color; legs dark brown or slaty brown.

Length, 4.10; wing, 2.30; tail, 1.85; tarsus, .75; bill, .45.

Habitat. Grand Cayman (type), Conception Island, Exuma Island, Rum Kay, Long Island, and Inagua.

This form is allied to *V. crassirostris*, but has the under parts yellow and the back dull olive-green.

SPECIES DESCRIBED SINCE 1880.

SPINDALIS ZENA TOWNSENDI. Ridgw.

TOWNSEND'S BAHAMA FINCH.

Spindalis zena townsendi. Ridgw., Proc. U. S. Nat. Mus., X., p. 3 (1887); Cory, Birds of the West Indies, p. 289 (1889).

SP. CHAR. — Described as being similar to *S. zena*, but with the back either entirely olive or much mixed with this color, instead of being uniform black. A somewhat doubtful form. Specimens from New Providence often have the back showing olive.

HABITAT. Abaco Island.

ICTERUS NORTHROPI. Allen.

NORTHROP'S ORIOLE.

Icterus northropi. Allen, Auk, p. 343 (1890).

Adult Male. — Whole anterior half of the body, as far as the middle of the breast below, and including the interscapulium above, together with the wings (except the lesser and median coverts) and tail, deep black; rest of the body, the thighs, lesser and median wing-coverts, edge of the wings, lower wing-coverts and axillars, rich lemon yellow; great wing-coverts and primaries very narrowly edged, and the outer tail-feathers very narrowly tipped with white; bill and feet black; lower mandible, with the basal third, bluish. In one specimen the longest two lower tail-coverts are mixed yellow and black. In the other specimens they are all wholly yellow.

Adult Female.— Similar to the male, except slightly smaller, and with the back a little less lustrous. (Allen, orig. descr., l. c.)

HABITAT. Andros Island.

AGELAIUS PHŒNICEUS BRYANTI. Ridgw.
BAHAMA RED-WINGED BLACKBIRD.

Agelaius phœniceus bryanti. Ridgway, Manual N. A. Birds, p. 370 (1887).

SP. CHAR. — Differs very slightly, if any, in coloration from *A. Phœniceus*, but is claimed to vary in its proportions, having the bill larger and the general size smaller.

DRYOBATES VILLOSUS MAYNARDI. Ridgw.
MAYNARD'S WOODPECKER.

Picus villosus. Bryant, Pr. Bost. Soc. Nat. Hist., VII., p. 106 (1859); Cory, Bds. Bahama, I., p. 120 (1880).

Picus insularis. Mayn., The Nat. in Florida, I., No. 4 (1885); not of Gould, 1862.

Picus villosus insularis. Cory, List Bds. W. I., p. 19 (1885).

Dryobates villosus maynardi. Ridgw., Man. N. A. Bds., p. 282 (1887); Cory, Birds of the West Indies, p. 170 (1889).

SP. CHAR. *Male.* — Above black, with a white band down the middle of the back, finely lined with black; all the quills, middle and larger wing-coverts with numerous spots of white; crown black; a patch over the eye, and a stripe from the mandible to the nape, white; a black stripe from the eye, passing through the cheeks, over the nape, and joining the black of the back; a scarlet crescent around the base of the skull, joining the white superciliary stripe; under parts ashy, with the sides mottled and striped with black; two outer tail-feathers white, edged and tipped with pale brown; third black, with a patch of pale brown upon the outer web; the others black.

Female. — The scarlet crescent wanting; replaced by white.

Length, 7.25; wing, 4.20; tail, 3; tarsus, .70; bill, 1.

HABITAT. Northern Bahama Islands.

This form differs from *D. villosus* in the greater extent of white in front of the eye, the black streaks on the sides of the breast, and black shaft lines on the white feathers of the back.

CENTURUS NYEANUS. Ridgw.

NYE'S WOODPECKER.

Centurus nyeanus. Ridgway, Auk, III., p. 336 (1886); Cory, Birds of the West Indies, p. 295 (1889).

"Similar to *C. superciliaris* of Cuba, but much smaller; the white bars of upper parts and gray of lower parts almost entirely devoid of yellow tinge; red of belly and black superciliary spot more restricted, and outer webs of middle tail-feathers without spots." — *Ridg., l. c.*

HABITAT. Watling's Island, Bahamas.

SPECIES DESCRIBED SINCE 1880.

CENTURUS BLAKEI. Ridgw.

BLAKE'S WOODPECKER.

Centurus blakei. Ridgw., Auk, III., p. 337 (1886); Cory, Birds of the West Indies, p. 296 (1889).

"Similar to *C. nyeanus*, but much darker; the forehead pale drab, or light grayish buff, instead of pure white; auriculars deep light drab, foreneck and chest olivaceous-drab, and lighter bars of black; scapulars and rump light dingy buff, instead of nearly pure white; frontlet, dull orange red, instead of pure vermilion or scarlet." — *Ridgw., l. c.*

HABITAT. Abaco Island.

COCCYZUS MAYNARDI. (Ridgw.)

MAYNARD'S CUCKOO.

Coccyzus maynardi. Ridgway, Manual of N. A. Birds, p. 274 (1887); Cory, Birds of the West Indies, p. 296 (1889).

Smaller and paler than *C. minor;* under parts buff or ashy, not ochraceous, as in *C. minor.*

HABITAT. Bahama Islands.

SPECIES DESCRIBED SINCE 1880.

RALLUS CORYI. *Maynard.*
Cory's Rail.

Rallus coryi. Maynard, American Exchange and Mart, Boston, Jan. 15 (1887); *Ib.,* Feb. 5 (1887); Cory, Birds of the West Indies, p. 254 (1889).

Sp. Char. — "Above pale yellowish brown, streaked with pale ashy; wings, light reddish brown, becoming paler on the outer edges; beneath pale ashy, tinged with reddish across the breast, becoming white on the throat and abdomen; banded faintly on sides and flanks with white and pale ashy." — *Maynard, l. c.*

Length, 11.45; wing, 5; tail, 2.35; tarus, 1.65.

Habitat. Andros Island.

ARDEA BAHAMENSIS. *Brewster.*
Bahama Green Heron.

Ardea bahamensis. Brewster, Auk, V., p. 83 (1888); Cory, Birds of the West Indies, p. 298 (1889).

Sp. Char. — Smaller than *A. virescens;* the general coloring much paler, browner, or yellower, and more uniform; the forehead strongly tinged with brownish; the light edging of the secondaries broader; the dorsal plumes and rump only slightly, sometimes not at all, greenish; top of head dark dull green, strongly tinged with brownish on the forehead; throat, jugulum, and foreneck creamy

SPECIES ADDED SINCE 1880.

white, with dusky spotting on the jugulum; remainder of head and neck light chestnut, approaching cinnamon in places; fore part and sides of back rusty cinnamon; rump and most of upper tail-coverts drab; dorsal plumes dull greenish, the central ones glaucous, with a tinge of lilac; wings and tail dull green, the wing-coverts edged broadly on both webs, the secondaries more narrowly on the outer webs only, with rusty or whitish under wing-coverts; breast, abdomen, crissum, and sides of the body, light yellowish drab." — *Brewster, orig. descr., l. c.*

HABITAT. Bahama Islands (Rum Kay, Watling's Island, Abaco Island).

This form is probably resident in the Bahamas. *A. virescens* is also common in the Bahamas, and extends throughout the West Indies.

SPECIES AND SUBSPECIES WHICH HAVE BEEN ADDED TO THE FAUNA SINCE 1880.

AMMODRAMUS SAVANNARUM. (Gmel.)

SOUTHERN YELLOW-WINGED SPARROW.

This species is recorded by Maynard as occurring in the Bahamas. (*Ammodramus australis mayn.*)

CORRECTIONS AND CHANGES SINCE 1880.

AMMODRAMUS SAVANNARUM PASSERINUS. (Wils.)
YELLOW-WINGED SPARROW.

This form has been taken in the Bahamas. Specimens from Andros Island and New Providence are in my collection.

LARUS ARGENTATUS. Brünn.
HERRING GULL.

A bird of this species was killed near Nassau during the winter of 1888, and another seen in January, 1889.

CORRECTIONS AND CHANGES WHICH HAVE BEEN MADE SINCE 1880, WITH REMARKS ON SEVERAL SPECIES WHICH SHOULD BE ELIMINATED.

MIMOCICHLA RUBRIPES. (Temm.)

This species is restricted to the island of Cuba, and we have no authentic record of its capture in the Bahamas. The specimens identified by Dr. Bryant as this species were probably *M. plumbea.*

LOXIGILLA NOCTIS. (Linn.)

This species, which was given by me as occurring in Inagua, is not found north of the Lesser Antilles. The specimens which I identified at that time as *L. noctis* were merely small examples of *L. violacea.*

CORRECTIONS AND CHANGES SINCE 1880.

SPINDALIS ZENA. (Linn.)

On page 93 mention is made of this species as occurring in Jamaica. Gosse writes of it as *S. zena*, but *S. zena* is restricted to the Bahamas; an allied species, *S. nigricephala*, being found in Jamaica.

SPORADINUS BRACEI. Lawr.

This type of *S. bracei* is a mummy, and the color of the feathers may have been slightly changed in consequence. It cannot be considered as separable from *S. recordii*.

SAUROTHERA BAHAMENSIS. Bryant.

This species is found on Andros Island and New Providence. A series of specimens from the former island appear to be slightly darker than the specimens from New Providence, but the color varies. On page 116, no mention is made of the white tail spots, which are one of the characters of the adult; the bird there described being an immature specimen. The adult bird, in breeding plumage, has a subterminal band of black on the tail-feathers, which are broadly tipped with white, excepting the two central ones, which only show a faint line of white on the extreme tips.

COLUMBIGALLINA PASSERINA. (Linn.)

Mr. Maynard separated the Bahama bird as paler and smaller than the mainland bird, and having the bill constantly wholly black. The form has since been found to be untenable, none of the characters being constant.

CORRECTIONS AND CHANGES SINCE 1880.

PANDION HALIÆTUS CAROLINENSIS. (Gmel.)

This osprey is common in the Bahamas. Mr. Maynard has described the Bahama bird as *P. ridgwayi;* but in a series of specimens I find no differences sufficient to warrant its separation from birds from the mainland.

ARDEA CYANIROSTRIS. Cory.

In originally describing this bird as new, I considered it distinct from *A. tricolor ruficollis* from the totally different coloration of the bill and legs, supposed to occur only in the breeding season. Since that time similar specimens have been taken in the winter season. *A. tricolor ruficollis* undoubtedly assumes a yellow bill during most of the year at least, even if Audubon was wrong in his statement to the effect that it had a partly yellow bill during the breeding season. It is probable that the two birds are identical, but it is also possible that the Bahama bird may be distinct; and colonies occasionally wander to Florida, where it has been found breeding. This would account for the blue-billed specimens being taken in Florida, and would not prove its identity with *A. tricolor ruficollis.*

CHANGES IN NOMENCLATURE AND CLASSIFICATION.

Mimus bahamensis = Mimus gundlachi. (Caban.
Mimus carolinensis = Galeoscoptes carolinensis. (Linn.)
Parula americana = Compsothlypis americana. (Linn.)
Dendroeca pinus = Dendroica vigorsii. (Aud.)
Dendroeca = Dendroica.
Certhiola bahamensis = Coereba bahamensis. (Reich.)
Hirundo horreorum = Chelidon erythrogastra. (Bodd.)
Hirundo cyaneoveridis = Callichelidon cyaneoviridis. (Bryant.
Cyanospiza ciris = Passerina ciris. (Linn.)
Cyanospiza cyanea = Passerina cyanea. (Linn.)
Phonipara bicolor = Euetheia bicolor. (Linn.)
Agelaeus phœniceus = Agelaius phoeniceus bryanti. Ridgw.
Tyrannus griseus = Tyrannus dominicensis. (Gmel.)
Myiarchus stolidus var. lucaysiensis = Myiarchus sagrae. (Gundl.
Picus villosus = Dryobates villosus maynardi. Ridgw.
Accipiter fuscus = Accipiter velox. (Wils.)
Falco communis = Falco peregrinus anatum. (Bonap.
Pandion haliaetus = Pandion haliaetus carolinensis. (Gmel.)
Zenaida amabilis = Zenaida zenaida. (Bonap.)
Chamaepelia passerina = Columbigallina passerina. (Linn.)
Ortyx virginianus = Colinus virginianus. (Linn.)
Squaterola helvetica = Charadrius squaterola. (Linn.)
Charadrius fulvus var. virginicus = Charadrius dominicus. Müll.
Strepsilas interpres = Arenaria interpres. (Linn.)

CHANGES IN NOMENCLATURE AND CLASSIFICATION.

Gallinago wilsoni = Gallinago delicata. (Ord.)
Tringa bonapartei = Tringa fuscicollis. Vieill.
Tringoides macularius = Actitis macularia. (Linn.)
Platalea ajaja = Ajaja ajaja. (Linn.)
Ardea leucogastra var. leucoprymna = Ardea tricolor ruficollis. (Gosse.)
Nyctiardea violacea = Nycticorax violaceus. (Linn.)
Porphyrio martinica = Ionornis martinica. (Linn.)
Fuligula affinis = Aythya affinis. (Eyton.)
Fuligula collaris = Aythya collaris. (Donor.)
Fuligula ferina var. americana = Aythya americana. (Eyton.)
Sula fiber = Sula sula. (Linn.)
Sula dactylatra = Sula cyanops. (Lunder.)
Graculus dilophus var. floridanus = Phalacrocorax dilophus floridanus. (Aud.)
Tachypetes aquilus = Fregata aquila. (Linn.)
Sterna anglica = Gelochelidon nilotica. (Hasselq.)
Sterna regia = Sterna maxima. Bodd.
Sterna cantiaca = Sterna sandvicensis acuflavida. (Cabot.)
Sterna paradisea = Sterna dougalli. Mont.
Sterna supercilliaris = Sterna antillarum. (Less.)
Oceanites oceanica = Oceanites oceanicus. (Kuhl.)
Puffinus obscurus = Puffinus auduboni. Finsch.
Podiceps dominicus = Colymbus dominicus. Linn.

PART I.

THE BAHAMA ISLANDS.

CHAPTER I.

THE BAHAMA ISLANDS.

The Bahama Islands are situated between 20° 55' and 27° 15' north latitude, and 78° 18' west longitude, comprising about a thousand islands, large and small, from Andros Island, which has an area of over a thousand square miles, to the small reef barely protruding from the surface of the sea, fit only for the occasional resting-place of some of the numerous sea birds which repair to these islands to breed. Nearly all the group present the same geological formation, being composed principally of cellular limestone. On most of the islands the rock along the shore has been worn away by the action of the sea in such a manner as to present a surface covered with sharp points, hard and keen as knife-blades, which renders walking an exceedingly difficult and sometimes dangerous operation, and a fall might be attended with serious consequences. Although so hard upon the surface, this stone, when not exposed to the atmosphere, is soft and easily cut, and is much used by the inhabitants for building purposes. It is an interesting fact to observe that this peculiar honeycombed appearance of the rocks is to be seen in the interior of some of the largest islands, showing that they were, in ages past, covered by the ocean.

Thousands of years ago, these beautiful islands were represented by the barren tops of submarine mountains, over which the waves dashed in the fury of the hurricane, or the calm expanse of water lay unbroken, hardly rippled by the gentle breezes of the tropics. Generation after generation of coral insects lived and died, working steadily, gradually raising the foundation of a future home for mankind. Ages passed, and their summits reached the surface, vegetation appeared, and now they stand, like oases in a desert, their tall palms swaying in the breeze, teaching us still another lesson in the beautiful work of creation.

Although in many places the soil is exceeding scant, yet vegetation flourishes on the larger islands. The cedar, lignumvitæ, satin-wood, mahogany, and many other species abound. Among the fruits, the banana, sapodilla, coffee-plant, tamarind, mango, guava, orange, cocoanut, marmee, shattuck, grape-fruit, and many others grow in profusion. Birds and fish abound, many of them very beautiful; but the zoölogy of the islands is limited. On some of the larger ones, wild cattle and hogs are numerous, but they are descendants of a few domestic representatives of their race which were imported years ago. No other animals were observed, except several species of mice and two species of bats.

On Andros Island the Iguana is abundant, and the natives consider it a great delicacy. Only one small one was seen by our party. Both the green turtle and the tortoise are common, and the shell of the latter forms an important item in the commerce of the islands. Crustacea and radiata are numerous, as well as land mollusks. The entomology is varied and interesting. Mosquitoes and such troublesome species are not common in winter except on the outer islands, where sand-flies are also numerous. Many species of lepidoptera and diptera abound throughout the group, especially during the summer season.

Many of the islands are infested with centipedes. At Nassau they were numerous, and occasionally a tarantula was seen, but the latter is by no means common, although during the hot summer months they, as well as curious and gigantic land-crabs, are to be found in abundance. About May 1st the heat begins to grow oppressive, and later it becomes almost unbearable, the mercury rising to 165° and even 170° in the middle of the day, when exposed to the heat of the sun; but, as a general rule, the mornings and evenings are very pleasant. I include below the average temperature, taken during the month of June while cruising among the islands. On cloudy days the sun temperature was not taken, and in nearly all cases being taken on the deck of the vessel, in all probability it was slightly affected by the breeze.

8 A. M.	12 Noon.	12 Noon.	6 P. M.
Shade.	Shade.	Sun.	Shade.
82	86½	118⅘	81½

Myriads of insects abound at this season, and render the southern islands almost uninhabitable. At Inagua we found them especially numerous and troublesome. The inhabitants stated that their horses were sometimes killed by them. This statement may be easily believed after having experienced the torture which they inflict, and seeing the animals literally covered with insects. The small keys which, during the winter, present a desolate appearance, in the summer season teem with bird life; thousands of Terns of different species repair to these deserted spots to breed, and their eggs might be gathered by the barrelful, as the rocks and sand are, in places, almost covered with them.

Inagua, besides being one of the largest islands of the Bahamas, is the most southern of the group. It is interesting to the sportsman and the naturalist on account of the numbers of animals and birds which are common there, but are rarely found on any of the other islands. A few miles from the coast the road comes out upon a large prairie, where wild cattle, horses, and asses are abundant. Back of Mathewstown, a large lake some twelve miles in length abounds with Ducks and marsh birds. Flamingoes are very abundant, and the inhabitants organize a party every year, discover their breeding-places, and gather many hundreds of their eggs. Among the birds interesting to the naturalist might be mentioned the Parrot, Spoonbill (which, in some places, is very abundant), and the little Humming-bird (*D. lyura*), which seems to be restricted to this island. The island of Inagua has never been fully explored, and would no doubt richly repay any naturalist who had the leisure and energy to complete the exploration of its interior.

Long Island and Eluthera are worthy of a visit on account of the natural caves which abound, some of them large and beautiful.

Numbers of skeletons and many specimens of wood-carving have been found in them. The negroes are superstitious, and rarely enter the caves alone; and so many which are known to exist are as yet unexplored. Clarence Harbor, Long Island, is a safe harbor, and the inhabitants very hospitable.

CHAPTER II.

NASSAU.

It was a bright and cloudless Christmas morning on which I first entered the harbor of Nassau, and as the ship came to an anchor off the bar, the bay presented a very pretty appearance; all the ships at anchor, as well as innumerable small craft, which were constantly passing and repassing, were covered with flags of all colors and nationalities. Upon the shore, just rising above the tops of a group of cocoanut-trees, the white spires of the city were plainly to be seen, their tops glistening in the reflected light of the first rays of the rising sun.

In a short time the ship was surrounded by a number of small boats, which flocked around us like birds of prey around some dead sea-monster, all anxious to carry away something for themselves. Each boatman was loud in the praises of his own boat, and a war of words was kept up, which showed no signs of abating as we slowly glided towards the wharf in the small craft which we had selected.

One of the first things that attracted our attention was the wonderful transparency of the water. Objects were plainly seen at a depth of fifteen feet, and, by the aid of an instrument which is called a water-glass, one can gaze down into the water and watch the fishes darting in and out among the many-colored "sea-ferns" and corals as clearly as if they were contained in an aquarium. Oftentimes, while cruising among the keys, I have sat gazing into the water, watching the countless varieties of fish which passed beneath us, from the immense shark, whose dull, brown body was just concealed beneath the surface, to the silver and angel fishes, which flashed and sparkled like rare gems as they lazily turned themselves in the sunlight or suddenly darted from some snug retreat formed by the beautiful and varied submarine vegetation, resembling a tropical garden in miniature.

We landed amongst a crowd of negroes, and, after refusing repeated offers of assistance, made our way to a venerable carriage, drawn by two lean horses, and directed the driver to take us to the hotel. Entering the town, we found the streets of an almost snowy whiteness, which, in the glare of the sun, is very dazzling to the eyes at first, but one soon gets used to it, and after a short time it is not at all troublesome.

Nassau is the capital of the Bahamas, and is in fact the only place of any size in the whole of the group. It boasts of a fair library and a fine hotel, The Royal Victoria, which is beautifully situated upon a small hill, and commands a fine view of the city and harbor. We were made very comfortable at the Sargent House, kept by Mr. Epes Sargent, and our stay there was made very pleasant by the kindness of himself and wife.

There are many pleasant drives in the vicinity of Nassau. Forts Charlotte, Montague, and Fincastle are all interesting to the tourist, and the roads leading to them are, in many places, picturesque and beautiful, shaded by groves of palms and cocoanut-trees, and commanding a fine view of the ocean and reefs. I was particularly pleased with the drive to Fort Montague. The air was perfumed by the myriads of flowers, which hung in festoons from the bushes or peeped above the thick growth of cacti bordering the road. We observed, as we drove along, many kinds of fruit growing in tropical luxuriance; among them might be enumerated the banana, pineapple, orange, sapodilla, cocoanut, and grape-fruits. Numbers of birds were chattering among the trees, while an occasional flash among the flowers revealed to the close observer the beautiful little Bahama Humming-bird, as it hovered for a moment before darting out of sight amongst the foliage. Near Fort Montague some very good bathing-houses have been erected, and a bath in the clear water during the cool of the evening is very refreshing.

Fort Fincastle, which is situated at the head of what is called "The Queen's Staircase," is a curious old structure, now gradually falling into decay. The staircase is one of the prettiest spots in Nassau, consisting of a flight of steps cut in the rock, which rises on both sides, in perpendicular walls, to the height of eighty or ninety feet. The rock is overhung with creeping vines, giving it the appearance of some moss-covered castle of feudal times, and the effect is heightened by the well-worn steps leading to the summit. When viewed from a certain position, the fort has the appearance of an old steamboat; a lookout which has been built upon it heightens the resemblance, as its position and appearance are that of a pilot-house.

To strangers visiting these islands for the first time, the habits and customs of the people are full of interest. The little negro boys, diving for pennies, or lining the wharves in a nude condition, hoping against hope for some one to throw them a penny, the tropical fruits of all kinds, and beautiful flowers in full bloom in midwinter, all seem strange at first; but barely a week passes before everything appears as natural as if they had seen just such things every day of their lives.

Nassau contains a large number of soldiers, most of them colored troops which have served in Africa, and nearly all of them are decorated. They promenade the streets with their medals worn conspicuously upon their breasts, filling the natives with awe and admiration; women bearing oranges, bananas, or sugar-cane walk about or stand upon corners, soliciting patronage; men, women, and children, having articles of food to dispose of, congregate every morning at what is called the market, and there offer their wares for sale. Fish are brought there alive, and exposed for sale in tanks, so that the purchaser may be sure of obtaining everything fresh.

Outside of its other attractions, the island of New Providence is of great interest to the ornithologist, as here may be obtained those exceedingly rare species, *Mimocichla plumbea* and *Geothlypis rostratus*. The former was so exceedingly rare that a short time ago only three or four specimens were known to be in existence. During my visits to the island I observed another species of this family, which, unfortunately, I was unable to procure. *G. rostratus* is also very rare, and has been classed as a variety of *G. treclia*. This would be accounted for by the extreme scarcity of specimens and the difficulty of procuring a series for proper examination and comparison.

Among the more common species which are to be found at New Providence might be enumerated the Purple Grosbeak or Spanish Paroquet, of the inhabitants (*Loxigilla violacea*), the Bahama Finch (*Spindalis zena*), and Honey Creeper (*Certhiola bahamensis*), which, next to the Bahama Sparrow (*Phonipara bicolor*), is the most common species. Anis are abundant everywhere, and it is seldom that during a drive outside of the city their clear whistle is not heard, as they perch upon the swaying branches of some tree, or hop along the ground, after the manner of our Grackles. The little Ground Dove (*C. passerina*) is abundant, and is an object of interest to the sportsman. While walking through the pineapple-fields, hundreds of them would rise on all sides of us. The large White-headed Pigeon and Key West Dove are also abundant at certain seasons of the year. Many years ago the Quail (*Ortyx virginianus*) was introduced, and has since multiplied, so that at the present time it has become quite numerous, generally frequenting the "pine barrens." The lakes abound with Teal, Duck, and Coot, which afford excellent sport to those inclined to shoot them.

The climate during the winter is magnificent, and many people afflicted with consumption regularly visit Nassau to regain their health. Fabulous stories are told of the wonderful recuperative powers of the atmosphere, most of which are mere fabrications; but there is no doubt that the people of Nassau enjoy one of the finest climates in the world, the temperature ranging between 65° and 85° from November until April.

CHAPTER III.

EXUMA KEYS.

JANUARY 6. — The sea was as calm as a mill-pond, hardly rippled by the light breeze, which was barely sufficient to propel our vessel with sufficient speed to prevent her drifting upon the reefs. We had arrived in sight of Highburn Key, and as we moved slowly along within a short distance of the shore, we examined it with the pleasant anticipation which any naturalist experiences upon the first sight of a little-known land. The island appeared deserted; not a bird was in sight, and the song of a single Mocking-bird, borne faintly to us from the interior, was the only sound that broke the almost perfect stillness. I had hoped to find birds abundant here, but after rambling over the key for several hours, and finding only a few Mocking birds and Honey Creepers, we returned to the boat, rather dissatisfied with our first excursion. These keys, although rarely visited, are very pretty. Cocoanuts and bananas abound, and can be generally obtained, conchs are abundant, and fair fishing is to be had; but these little islands, which, later in the season, are fairly covered with bird life, are almost deserted in winter.

Norman's Key, Shroud Key, etc., passed in succession, showing the same geological formation and desolate appearance. On some of them, birds were common, but appeared to be confined to two or three species. On Norman's Key, wild hogs are abundant, and afford good sport; but dogs are required to hunt them successfully. Cattle were at one time also found here, but of late years none have been seen. Among these keys sponges are very plentiful, and are much sought after by the negroes; hardly a day passed without our meeting one or more of their small boats. In gathering the sponges, the negroes use an instrument resembling an eel-spear, having a strong iron prong attached to the end of a stout pole, with which they detach the sponges from the rocks. They also use a "water-glass," a simple construction, made in the shape of an oblong box, one end being closed by a pane of glass, leaving the other end open. By holding the glass end submerged, small objects can easily be seen at the depth of fifteen or twenty feet. Many of the negroes are very expert divers, and descend thirty-five or forty feet, and often much deeper, in search of the finer qualities of sponges, which are only to be found in deep water. Although sharks are very numerous, the negroes do not seem to mind them in the least, and enter the water anywhere with perfect impunity.

We had expected to find water-birds very abundant, but were disappointed. Marsh-birds were also scarce, although the long beaches and numerous marshes seemed to offer excellent feeding-grounds. We procured a few scattered birds of different species, but were not sorry when one morning, a few days later, finding birds as scarce as ever, and having a fair wind, we turned our backs on the keys and directed our course for Andros, that much-talked-of but little-known island.

The wind increased to a strong breeze, and, soon after starting, the land we had left became an indistinct line in the distance, which gradually faded from our view, until we rolled upon an unbroken sea of white-capped waves, which occasionally sent their spray high over the deck. About noon we sighted Green Key, and passed within a stone's throw of the shore. A flock of Royal Terns, which were sunning themselves upon the beach, rose with harsh cries, and circled and played around us until Green Key, in turn, had sunk in the horizon, and the low shores of Andros Island appeared in the distance, heralded by the rumbling thunder of the waves breaking upon the coral reefs. A few minutes later, our little vessel rounded to, and entered a small, rock-bound harbor, startling a number of Cormorants, which flapped hurriedly away as we dropped our anchor in the still water.

CHAPTER IV.

ANDROS ISLAND.

Andros Island is the largest of the Bahama group, being about ninety miles long, and from ten to forty miles in width. It is thickly wooded, and intersected by a number of broad, shallow creeks. An extensive fresh-water lake exists in the interior, which abounds in all kinds of birds, and is well worthy of a visit, although it is rather difficult to get at. It may be reached by the Wide Opening from the west side, or Fresh Creek from the east; but the latter is too shallow, near its head, to admit of reaching the lake the entire way by boat, and a "carry" of several miles will have to be made.

There are no good harbors; but small craft, not drawing more than four or five feet of water, will easily find their way through the reefs on the eastern side of the island, but on the west side it is so shallow that even small vessels cannot approach within miles of the shore. On the shallow flats, quantities of birds congregate yearly, and Flamingoes, Pelicans, etc., are said to abound. Iguanas are numerous in the interior, and their flesh is much esteemed by the negroes, who prefer it to any other kind of meat.

On the southern portion of the island many valuable kinds of trees grow in abundance; among them we observed the ebony (scarce), mahogany, lignumvitæ, cedar, logwood, and many others, which would prove a mine of wealth to any one able to master the difficulties of their transportation to the coast. I was told that ambergris used to be found in considerable quantities along the shores, but is now scarce. Several species of birds were taken on this island which we did not find elsewhere. Among them were the rare Kirtland's Warbler (*Dendroeca kirtlandii*) and the beautiful little Humming-bird (*Sporadinus recordi*).

Sandpipers, Plovers, Tattlers, Oyster-catchers, etc., were abundant. Turkey Buzzards were common, and it is a curious fact that although this species is very plentiful on Andros Island and at Abaco, none are to be found on the other islands, except, perhaps, an occasional straggler.

The island presents about the same appearance throughout; its rocky shore is inhabited only by a few settlements of negroes, who live in the most primitive manner, in their thatch-roofed houses, surrounded by their cocoanuts and bananas, seeming as happy and contented as possible. The people are friendly and obliging, and, for a small consideration, will make themselves very useful to the sportsman.

Although there are several good-sized villages on the eastern shore of the island, as there are no white inhabitants, provisions are very difficult to procure. Even eggs are scarce, and command a high price, the negroes often coming off to the vessel, bringing one or two eggs carefully packed in leaves, for which they demand from four to five cents apiece. Fruit can be obtained everywhere. We often purchased bunches of bananas for twenty or twenty-five cents which were so large as to require all our strength to lift them; and other fruits were proportionately cheap.

CHAPTER V.

LONG ISLAND. — THE CAVES.

CLARENCE HARBOR, June 7, 1879. — Objects had just begun to be distinguishable in the faint light of early dawn when we left the vessel and were pulled slowly to the shore. The morning was deliciously cool, and a thick mist hung over the water, through which, as we approached the beach, we could just discern our man Sam, keeping guard over four horses, which were destined to greatly assist us during the many hard journeys which we afterwards found it necessary to make.

My friend and myself selected our animals, and after seeing the provisions, ropes, etc., packed safely upon the backs of the others, we started in search of a large and little-known cave, which our guide was certain he could find, and which was situated, according to his statement, about ten miles from the village. The first part of the road was in fair condition for horses going at a slow pace, and at that hour the air was cool and refreshing, and the ride very enjoyable. Riding along the edge of a small inland pond, I observed numbers of birds which would have gladdened the heart of any naturalist. Gull-billed Terns and Black-headed Gulls circled around us or poised themselves over the pond, with bent heads, gazing intently at its unbroken surface, several long-legged Stilts stood in solemn silence in the shallow water, and a number of little Nighthawks still darted hurriedly about in pursuit of insects. Occasionally, a Heron rose from its resting-place and flapped silently away, while the air was filled with the notes of birds and the hum of insects. As the day advanced, the chatter of the birds gradually ceased, and a perfect silence replaced the tumult of the morning, broken only by the occasional rattling of our horses' hoofs among the loose stones of the pathway,—it could hardly be called a road, although at one time it must have been a fine driveway. On either side were the remains of heavy stone walls, occasionally broken by huge pillars, which marked the entrance to some grand old mansion, represented by an over-grown ruin, its once beautiful grounds now thickly covered by an almost impenetrable growth of semi-tropical vegetation. As the sun rose higher and higher, the heat became intense, and our discomfort was greatly increased by the myriads of mosquitoes and other small insects which attacked us incessantly. The horses suffered badly from them, the poor creatures fidgeting and turning their heads in a supplicating way, as if to ask us to relieve them of their tormentors.

After travelling for several hours over an exceedingly bad road, which grew worse and worse as we advanced, we at last arrived at an opening in the side of a small hill, which the guide declared to be the mouth of the cave. Here we dismounted, and leaving our man to attend to the tired horses, we lighted our torches and, followed by Sam bearing the ropes and extra lights, entered the opening and found ourselves in a large gallery, extending, with a gradual curve to the left, as far as we could see. A few yards from the entrance, a passage turned suddenly to the right, through a small opening barely large enough to admit of the passage of a man's body, while the main gallery continued on to the left, gradually growing higher as we advanced. Choosing the small opening, we entered, and made our way along a narrow passage for a short distance, when it suddenly turned and opened into a large chamber, which presented, as we entered it, one of the most beautiful sights that I have ever seen. It was about thirty feet wide, and the walls, which appeared pure white, were smooth and sloped gradually inward, forming a dome-shaped ceiling, hung with an intricate network of stalactites, which sparkled and glistened in the wavering light of the torches. Limestone pillars, of all shapes and sizes, rose from floor to ceiling, some of them as yet imperfectly formed, while others appeared as thick as the trunks of large trees. It was easy for one to imagine himself in the council-chamber of some mighty king of a long-forgotten race, and the effect was heightened by a recess in the wall, which had the appearance of an immense chair. In a passage leading from this chamber was found a large skeleton, lying in a narrow cavity of the rock, the head resting upon the right arm in a perfectly easy and natural position, as if death had occurred while sleeping. The skeleton was evidently that of a very large man, who, when alive, must have stood nearly seven feet in height. The skull was curiously formed, having the frontal bone much flattened, evidently by artificial means, and the upper jaw protruding in such a manner that the man's face, when alive, must have had a frightful expression. Retracing our steps, we entered the main gallery, and followed it for about fifty yards, when another passageway was discovered at right angles with the one we were following. It extended but a short distance, leading to a small chamber, hung with a few stalactites, but not to be compared with the one we had first entered. A number of small passages led away in different directions, but few of them large enough to permit of our entrance; and those which we were able to enter were gradually being closed by the almost imperceptible growth of the huge pillars.

This cave, as far as we were able to enter it, appeared to be about two hundred yards in depth. Some of the chambers literally swarmed with bats, which flew about our heads or hung from the ceiling, uttering shrill squeaks as we penetrated into their domain.

As we emerged from the cave, it seemed like entering an oven. Our animals stood with drooping heads and half-closed eyes, seemingly overcome by the intense heat. The mercury exposed to the sun showed a temperature of 154°, and if a foot was exposed for a few minutes to the sun's rays, the shoe became so hot as to cause a burning sensation to the skin. Our drinking-water, which had been put up in bottles and packed in the saddle-bags, was found to have become *hot*. Both of us had a slight headache, but there was no help for it. It was either go on, or miss visiting some of the other caves, which the guide claimed were in close proximity; so we mounted our distressed animals, and made our way slowly along the path leading to a cave which a negro had lately discovered, but which had not been explored, the negroes being very superstitious regarding the caves, and rarely entering one alone if it can be avoided. As we rode, the perspiration fairly dripped from our faces, although we were moving at a slow walk, causing us no exertion whatever. Soon the path became so bad that the horses could go no farther, so we had to dismount and follow our guide on foot. He led us over rocks and through tangled vines for about a quarter of a mile, until at last we came to what appeared to be a well, descending perpendicularly for about twelve feet, which he stated was the entrance to the cave. Into this opening we descended, by the aid of a rope, and found ourselves in a large, low chamber, extending in all directions as far as we could see. It was so low that it was necessary to move about in a stooping position, at times crawling on the hands and knees. The floor was perfectly smooth and level, and of a rich brown color, being composed of a deep deposit of guano. After penetrating for some distance, and finding nothing of interest, we turned about and made our way back to the entrance. The air outside was cool in comparison with the oven-like temperature of the narrow passages through which we had crawled, and it was with a feeling of relief that, upon reaching the place where we had left the horses, we once more mounted them and turned their heads homeward.

After riding for some time, we came upon a small hut, which offered a comparatively cool shelter, and feeling that it would be unsafe to proceed farther during the heat of the day, we led the tired animals to a shady corner, and stretching ourselves upon the stone floor, alternately smoked and slept until the sun had disappeared behind the hills in the distance. A refreshing breeze had sprung up, and as our horses were somewhat rested, we remounted, and an hour later entered the village of Clarence Harbor, and fired a gun as a signal to notify the men on board the vessel of our arrival. In a few minutes the dim outline of the boat appeared, and half an hour later, seated in the cabin enjoying a good supper, the fatigue of the day was forgotten. Supper over, we went on deck, and stretching ourselves in the large easy-chairs, enjoyed our cigars while watching the waves, lit up by myriads of animalculæ, seeming on fire as they dashed against the side of the vessel.

While at Clarence Harbor, a negro brought me a curiously carved piece of lignumvitæ-wood which he had found in a cave, far back in the hills, while exploring for guano. The wood was cut to represent a tortoise, having a human head, but with the back hollowed out instead of being oval, and was evidently carved from one piece of wood. It had been in his possession for over a year, and placing no value upon it, the head had been broken off and lost, and the body somewhat injured, he having allowed his children to use it as a plaything. In spite of the reward which I offered him, he was unable to find the missing parts, and so another valuable and interesting specimen was destroyed through ignorance.

CHAPTER VI.

THE MIRAPORVOS.

The group of islands known as Miraporvos are situated about fifteen miles west of Castle Rock, Acklin Island, and are simply a number of small, barren reefs, the largest of them not exceeding half a mile in extent.

It is dangerous to attempt to visit them, as there are many concealed reefs in their vicinity, and, as there is no harbor whatever, the vessel is compelled to come to anchor under the lee of the island, and be kept in readiness to put to sea at once, if the wind should change. As we approached the islands, immense quantities of Terns were flying about or resting upon the water, and among them we observed a number of Shearwaters and Booby Gannets.

Upon landing, we found the whole island covered with a thick growth of cactus, which made walking rather uncomfortable, as the sharp needles cut through the clothes, and drew blood freely. As we advanced, hundreds of Terns rose upon all sides of us, uttering harsh cries as they flew about our heads, while others nearly allowed themselves to be stepped on before they offered to leave the nest.

Near the middle of the island there is a small marsh, which we found tenanted by a number of Waders, of different species. Several Wilson Plovers seemed greatly disconcerted by our presence, and showed such evident signs of anxiety that I was certain that their eggs could not be far off; but although we searched diligently for them, we were unable to find a single egg. Meanwhile, the Plovers had been flying about us, uttering short, sharp notes of distress, but, upon our moving away, they immediately ceased their lamentations, and became as quiet as possible, evidently satisfied that we had given up the search. While walking through the short marsh-grass, a Dove suddenly started up from almost under my feet, which I recognized as the little Ground Dove (*C. passerina*); but, to be positive, I shot the bird, and then commenced a careful search for the nest, and was lucky enough to find it without any trouble. It was simply a little mat of sticks, on which were deposited two beautiful little white eggs, which were quite fresh.

Yellow-crowned Night Herons (*N. violacea*) were very abundant; we must have started over a hundred of them during our circuit of the island, and I was enabled to procure a number of their rare eggs, sometimes finding two or three nests on the same bush.

We found Terns more abundant on this island than anywhere else in the Bahamas, and as it is an unfrequented spot, they are so tame as to often allow themselves to be taken from the nest without offering to fly. Several of the men whom I sent on shore brought back a number of the birds alive, and several basketsful of eggs, mostly those of Terns and Night Herons. Some of them were cracked, and they requested me to allow them to have them to eat. If they ate them, as I suppose they did, it was in all probability the most valuable omelet they will ever have set before them, the eggs of the Yellow-crowned Night Heron often selling as high as three dollars apiece.

It had been my intention to make quite a long stay at this island, as it offered a fine field for the investigation of the habits of several imperfectly known species; but on the evening of the second day after our arrival, the sky became overcast with heavy, black clouds, the wind suddenly changed, and as it would be unsafe to remain where we were in case of bad weather, we made all haste to weigh anchor and put to sea. An hour later, the storm reached us, but we were clear of the dangerous ground, and scudded before it, close-reefed, in the direction of Inagua.

CHAPTER VII.

INAGUA.

MATHEWSTOWN, which can boast of being the only white settlement on the island, resembles Nassau on a small scale. A good deal of salt is manufactured here, and the quantity exported every year is considerable for the size of the place. Cocoanut groves are being started, and, on the whole, the island is in a prosperous condition.

About ten miles back of Mathewstown there is a large lake, which, we had been told, was fairly alive with game at all seasons of the year, and to see this wonderful lake had been one of the main objects of my visit. On the next day after our arrival, we spent the afternoon arranging for the trip. In the evening the boats were placed upon small carts, barely large enough to hold them, which were to be drawn by small but strong donkeys, guns were cleaned, ammunition looked over, and everything prepared for an early start the next morning.

May 27.— It was three o'clock, and so dark that the outline of the shore was barely visible by the dim light of the stars, when we left the vessel. Some time was spent in getting everything arranged, but it was still dark when the sleepy negro, who was to act the part of driver, announced everything in readiness to start.

Climbing into the wagon, we were borne slowly along over a smooth road, which wound in and out through a labyrinth of salt-ponds, dotted here and there by small windmills, of a very primitive pattern, which are used in pumping water in and out of the ponds, sometimes taking a week to do what a small donkey-engine would accomplish in a few hours.

The road was quite good, and on the way we had a fine view of the country, which, in some places, extends in an unbroken prairie for miles. In such places, we observed numbers of wild asses. These pretty little creatures stood and gazed timidly at us as we passed, but the moment we made a movement towards them, away they went like the wind. One who has never seen the ass in its wild state, cannot appreciate the grace and beauty of these pretty little animals. Cattle and horses are also abundant on the island, in a wild state, and offer excellent sport. They are descendants of domestic animals, brought to the island many years ago.

The ride to the lake occupied several hours, and we were continually annoyed by myriads of mosquitoes and other insects. The road was covered by an immense quantity of land-crabs, most of them small, which hurriedly ran out of the way as we approached.

We found the lake, which is some twelve miles in extent, exceedingly shallow, rarely exceeding four feet in depth. Far out in the shallow water were several large flocks of Flamingoes, their scarlet plumage blazing brightly in the light of the morning sun. Pelicans were abundant, and Stilts, Willets, and a number of species of Sandpipers were continually flying about. I procured several specimens of the pretty little Bahama Duck (*Dafila bahamensis*), which we found quite abundant on the island, and I was also lucky enough to find two of their nests on a small island a short distance from the shore. Near the upper part of the lake is the largest Flamingo breeding-ground in the Bahamas. These birds repair to about the same place regularly every year, and breed in great numbers. The nest resembles a sugar-loaf in form, composed of clay and mud, having a slight depression in the top in which they deposit their eggs. Occasionally, during the rainy season, the water overflows the nests, and thousands of eggs are destroyed, many of which are washed ashore on the other side of the lake. I picked up a number on the beach which had evidently been in the water for a long time. Flamingoes' eggs are considered very good eating, and are much esteemed by the inhabitants, who, every year, organize a party and gather them in large quantities.

By noon, the heat had become excessive, and the birds which we had already killed, although dead but a few hours, and not exposed to the sun, already showed signs of decomposition; so, for fear of losing them, we hurriedly gathered our things together and started on the return trip to Mathewstown, where we arrived at sunset, tired and heated, but well pleased with our day's jaunt.

At Inagua, I found many species of birds which I did not find on any of the other islands. The Spoonbill is abundant in the creeks in many parts of the island, generally frequenting the mangroves. From fifty to a hundred were sometimes seen together, but they were shy, and difficult to approach. The Thrush (*Margarops fuscatus*), Parrot (*C. collaria*), Little Mocking-bird (*Mimus orpheus var. dominicus*), and Lyre Humming-bird (*Doricha lyura*) we also obtained here, and did not observe them elsewhere.

MEASUREMENT OF SPECIMENS.

WRITERS often differ in their style of measuring a specimen, and for that reason I include below the usual rules for measurement, which are followed in the present work.

LENGTH. — Distance, *in a straight line*, from the end of the bill to the tip of the longest tail-feather. Sometimes one or two feathers are much longer than the others, as in the Tropic bird.

WING. — Distance, *in a straight line*, from the carpus (bend of the wing) to the tip of the longest primary.

TAIL. — Distance from the body to the end of the longest feather.

BILL. — Distance, *in a straight line* (not taking the curve of the bill), from the tip to where it joins skin or feathers on the forehead. (Exception, birds having frontal plate.)

TARSUS. — Distance, *in front*, from the knee-joint to the root of the middle toe.

All measurements are given in inches, unless otherwise stated.

WORKS AND PAPERS REFERRED TO.

"Gosse," Philip Henry. Birds of Jamaica. 1 vol.

"Wils."—Wilson, Alexander. American Ornithology. 3 vols.

"Aud."—Audubon, John James. Birds of America. 7 vols.

"Bd.," "Bwr.," and "Ridg."—Baird, Brewer, and Ridgeway. North American Birds. 3 vols.

"Gld."—Mon. Trochil. Gould, John. Monograph of the Trochilidæ. 5 vols.

"Bryant."—Bryant, Henry. A List of Birds seen at the Bahamas from Jan. 20 to May 14, 1859. Proceedings of the Boston Society of Natural History. Vol. VII. p. 102.

"Bryant."—Bryant, Henry. Description of two Birds from the Bahama Islands hitherto undescribed. Proceedings of the Boston Society. Vol. IX. p. 279.

"Bryant."—Bryant, Henry. Additions to the List of Birds seen at the Bahamas. Proceedings of the Boston Society. Vol. XI. p. 63.

"Lawr."—Lawrence, George N. Descriptions of new Species of Birds of the Family Trochilidæ and Tetraonidæ. Annals of the New York Academy of Sciences. Vol. I. p. 50.

Moore, N. B. List of Birds, chiefly Visitors from North America, seen and killed in the Bahamas. Proceedings of the Boston Society. Vol. XIX. p. 241.

ABBREVIATIONS OF AUTHORS' NAMES.

Aud.	Audubon.	*Lafr.*	Lafresnaye.
Bd.	Baird.	*Lawr.*	Lawrence.
Bodd.	Boddaert.	*Licht.*	Lichtenstein.
Bp.	Bonaparte.	*Reich.*	Reichenbach.
Cab.	Cabanis.	*Ridg.*	Ridgeway.
Cass.	Cassin.	*Scl.*	Sclater.
Cs.	Coues.	*Sw.*	Swainson.
Gamb.	Gambel.	*Temm.*	Temminck.
Gld.	Gould.	*Vieil.*	Vieillot.
Gm.	Gmelin.	*Wagl.*	Wagler.
Gr.	Gray.	*Wils.*	Wilson.
Linn.	Linnæus.		

PART II.

BIRDS OF THE BAHAMA ISLANDS.

FAM. TURDIDÆ.

THRUSHES.

MIMOCICHLA PLUMBEA. (*Linn.*)
PLUMBEOUS THRUSH.

Local Name.— Blue Thrasher.

Adult Male.— General plumage, plumbeous; chin and small patch at base of lower mandible, white; throat, black; primaries and secondaries, dark brown, except the first two, edged with slaty gray; tail, very dark brown, almost black; the terminal third of the inner webs of the first two, and tips of first four feathers, white; crissum, plumbeous; legs and eyelids, vermilion red; iris, reddish brown.

Adult Female.— Similar to the male, but appears to be slightly smaller. Cannot be distinguished otherwise than by dissection.

Length 10.25, wing 5, tail 5, tarsus 1, bill .90.

For years, the Plumbeous Thrush has been represented only by a very few specimens in some of the large museum collections, and was considered so rare that I was very much surprised, upon visiting the Bahamas, to find it abundant on some of the islands.

At New Providence and Abaco, it was especially common, and I was enabled to collect a fine series of specimens. It generally remains concealed in the thickets, and, perhaps, for that reason, is seldom seen, although it is well known to the inhabitants by the name of Blue Thrasher. Its song is very pretty, at times resembling the notes of our common Robin (*Turdus migratorius*). The stomachs of several specimens contained the remains of berries and insects.

MIMOCICHLA RUBRIPES. (*Temm.*)
RED-LEGGED THRUSH.

Adult Male. — Chin and cheek striped white; throat, black, reaching upper breast; *belly, reddish brown,* deepest near the vent; *crissum, dull white;* three outer tail-feathers tipped with white.

Length about 11, wing 5, tail 4, bill .96.

The Red-legged Thrush has a general resemblance to the preceding species, but may be easily distinguished from it by the coloration of the belly and crissum.

I have never observed this species in the Bahamas, but have included it on the authority of Dr. Bryant, who claims to have met with three specimens in the neighborhood of Nassau, and says that the inhabitants knew it by the name of Blue Jay and Blue Thrasher. If this species does occur in the Bahamas, they no doubt consider it identical with the last species, and recognize both birds by the same name.

MARGAROPS FUSCATUS. (Vieil.)

PAW-PAW THRUSH.

Local Name. — Paw-paw Bird.

Adult Male. — Above, brown, the feathers slightly edged with ash; throat and breast, brown; feathers heavily edged with white, giving a mottled appearance, which shows faintly on the belly and almost disappears at the vent; primaries, brown, pale-edged; upper tail-coverts tipped with white; tail, brown, tipped with white; bill, yellowish, with an olive tinge; upper mandible shading into brown at the base; legs, pale olive; iris, pale yellow.

Length 10.25, wing 5.20, tail 4.50, tarsus, 1.40, bill .76.

This interesting species inhabits Inagua, but, as far as I was able to observe, it is not found on any of the other islands. All attempts to discover its nest were unsuccessful, and as it was not at all common, I am unable to state anything, from personal observation, regarding its habits. The natives at Northwest Point seemed to be well acquainted with it, and told me that the Paw-paw Bird was not uncommon in the interior of the island, and that its nest is built in hollow trees.

MIMUS ORPHEUS VAR. DOMINICUS. (*Linn.*) (*Bryant*)

LITTLE MOCKING-BIRD.

Adult Male.—Above, grayish brown, showing ashy on the back; under parts, white, slightly tinged with ashy on the breast; wings, brown; all of the primaries heavily marked with, and the eighth and ninth almost entirely, white; tail, brown, having the first two and entire inner web of third feathers white; bill, black; legs, brownish. Sexes similar.

Length 8.50, wing 4, tail 4.20, tarsus 1.20, bill .64.

This pretty little Mocking-bird, which is about the smallest of its family, is common at Inagua, and a constant resident. I have never met with it on any of the other islands, although the negroes claim that a small bird of this genus is occasionally seen on Long Island during the summer. Dr. Bryant found it at Inagua, but did not meet with it elsewhere in the Bahamas. It may be easily recognized by its small size and distinct wing-markings.

MIMUS BAHAMENSIS. (*Bryant.*)

BAHAMA MOCKING-BIRD.

Winter Plumage, Male.—Much larger than *M. polyglottus*, and the white tail-feathers wanting. Above, pale rufous-brown, the rufous tint most marked on the rump and upper tail-coverts; below, pale ash, streaked with fine lines of brown, becoming broader upon the sides; wings, rufous-brown, feathers slightly edged with pale rufous; wing-coverts tipped with white, forming two narrow bars; tail, dark brown, slightly tipped with dull white, wanting on the two middle feathers; legs, bluish black; bill, black; iris, yellow. The female resembles the male.

Length about 11, wing 5, tail 5, tarsus 1.60, bill .90.

This beautiful songster makes its home among the Bahama Islands, where it is very abundant throughout the year. Upon landing upon Highburn Key I observed a large bird clinging to the top of a small branch, which swayed about in the light breeze. It had the appearance of a Mocking-bird, but was much larger than any I had ever seen. As I looked, it lifted its head and uttered a series of notes such as I had rarely if ever heard equalled by any of our songsters. As it sung, gently swaying from one side to the other, it would suddenly cease, and then softly commence again, gradually increasing in power until it seemed carried away by the beauty of its own melody.

Dr. Bryant, during his visits to the Bahamas, found it very abundant. He says, "On those keys, which are barely large enough for any land birds to inhabit them, this bird is sure to be the first settler; and in some of them, as Ship Channel Keys, for instance which are only a few acres in extent, there would be two or three pairs, each occupying its own domain, which they did not allow to be invaded by the others without giving battle at once. It was singular, as well as pleasing, to see and hear on one of these lonely and almost desert keys, this graceful bird, mounted on the topmost spray of some dwarf shrub, singing with as much fervor and satisfaction as if surrounded by listeners, instead of having for sole auditor his faithful mate. The pairs seem to keep together after the period of incubation has passed, as all I met with, as early as February, were mated, and the inhabitants stated that they did not lay before May; and the sexual organs of all those dissected by me showed no appearance of excitement. In its habits it differs very much from our common species, delighting as much in solitude as the latter does in the society of mankind. Its food, during my visit, consisted almost entirely of the fruit of the prickly pear, with the addition of an occasional insect. I presume that the insectivorous part of its diet is proportionally greater when it inhabits the larger islands, but on the barren keys, on which I procured my specimens, insects are almost unknown, at least if I am to judge from the number seen by myself. The stomachs of all those procured by me contained a quantity of the seeds of the prickly pear, and a few remains of insects; and the feathers near the bill of all of them were stained red by the juice of the fruit."

None were observed on the island of New Providence by our party, although there is no reason why they should not be found there, and the inhabitants claim that they are occasionally met with in the vicinity of Nassau, but only on rare occasions.

MIMUS CAROLINENSIS. (Linn.)
CATBIRD.

Winter Plumage, Male. — Smaller and lighter colored than the northern bird. Above, dark slate color; crown and tail, black; under parts, pale slate color; crissum, chestnut; bill and legs, black. The female does not differ from the male, but is somewhat smaller.

Length about 7.90, wing 3.50, tarsus 1, bill .66.

The Catbird, although probably a regular winter visitant, is not very abundant, and we obtained but few specimens. Its habits appeared to me to be the same as when it visits the United States in the summer season. It undoubtedly wanders all over the islands. Dr. Henry Bryant obtained it at Inagua. This bird has received its name from its peculiar notes, which somewhat resemble the cry of a cat, and which it constantly utters while seeking for its food among the thick underbrush. Its food consists of insects, and berries of various kinds.

Fig. Aud. Bds. N. A., Vol. II. pl. 140.

FAM. SYLVIIDÆ.

POLIOPTILA CÆRULEA. (*Linn.*)

BLUE-GRAY GNAT-CATCHER.

Winter Plumage, Female.— Above, grayish blue; under parts and lores, bluish white; quills edged with bluish gray, becoming whiter on the tertials; two outer tail-feathers white, becoming black at the base, and extending obliquely forward on the inner webs; third tail-feather tipped with white, the others black.

Adult Male.—With a narrow frontal line of black, extending over the eye; otherwise resembles the female.

Length 4.40, wing 2, tail 2.20, tarsus .70, bill .40.

This little species is a resident of the Bahamas, although much less abundant in summer than in winter, as their numbers become greatly augmented during the latter season by migrants from the United States. When we arrived at Inagua they were quite abundant, and evidently breeding; so, being very desirous of procuring the eggs of this species, I watched them carefully, and was rewarded by finding a nest containing three eggs, on June 1st, the eggs being all quite fresh. The nest was a beautiful little structure, built in the crotch of a diminutive palm-tree, about four feet from the ground. The old birds were very tame, the male perching himself upon the end of a twig, not two feet from my hand, and singing away as merrily as possible, seemingly with the intention of attracting me away from the nest. I never had heard before a bird of this species utter such varied and pleasing song. The poor little female fluttered anxiously around me, and upon my removing the nest, she hopped down into the crotch where it had rested, and after peering about for a few seconds, seemed in such distress that I was almost tempted to replace the nest and leave her in the happy possession of her treasures.

It is a curious fact that, during the month of January, out of a series of some fifty specimens which were shot and examined, only a single male bird was taken; but later in the season, the males and females seemed to be about equally distributed.

Dr. Bryant found this species very abundant at Inagua.

Fig. Aud. Bds. N. A., Vol. I. pl. 70.

FAM. SYLVICOLIDÆ.

WARBLERS.

MNIOTILTA VARIA. (Linn.)
BLACK AND WHITE CREEPER.

Winter Plumage, Male.—Upper parts, black, the feathers broadly edged with brownish white; a superciliary line of brownish white; under parts, white, with faint ash-colored stripes upon the sides of the breast, shading into brownish upon the sides of the belly and crissum; two clearly defined bands upon the wings; tail, black, edged with whitish; inner webs of the two outer tail-feathers tipped with white.

Female.—Similar to the male, having the under parts white, faintly marked with blackish on the sides.

Length 5.05, wing 2.75, tail 2.10, tarsus .80, bill .50.

The Black and White Creeper is not uncommon during the winter on some of the larger islands. I procured specimens during December and January, and Dr. Bryant found it common from April 20 to May 10. It has a curious habit of climbing the trunks of trees, after the manner of Woodpeckers, searching diligently for the numerous insects which it finds concealed in the interstices of the bark. None were seen after May 7.

Fig. Aud. Bds. N. A., Vol. II. pl. 114.

PARULA AMERICANA. (Linn.)
BLUE YELLOW-BACKED WARBLER.

Winter Plumage, Male. — Above, blue; a slight tinge of yellow upon the crown and nape; middle of the back with a broad patch of greenish yellow; throat and breast, yellow, with an imperfect band of blue across the jugulum anterior to one of brown intermixed with yellow; a small white spot on the eyelid; sides of the head, ashy blue; two well-defined white bands on the wings; belly, white, shading into ash upon the sides and flanks, and yellowish upon the crissum; tail, with the exception of the two middle feathers, showing a patch of white upon the inner webs.

Winter Plumage, Female. — Above, olive; under parts, dull white, sometimes showing a tinge of brownish on the breast.

Length 4.40, wing 2.35, tail 2, tarsus .65.

Not uncommon during the winter. All the specimens procured were taken at Nassau, N. P., but there is no doubt that it ranges throughout the islands, as it is known to have a much greater southern range than the Bahamas. Dr. Bryant found it common during his visit to these islands in 1866.

All the specimens obtained by me were killed among the small trees bordering the road; but none were seen in the "pine barrens," where other species of its family were abundant. None remain later than April.

Fig. Aud. Bds. N. A., Vol. II. pl. 91.

HELMITHERUS VERMIVORUS. (Gm.)
WORM-EATING WARBLER.

Adult Male. — Above, olive-green; head striped with yellowish brown and black on each side of the crown, which is brownish yellow; under parts, pale brownish yellow, dull on the belly, and tinged with olive on the sides.

Adult Female. — Resembles the male, but having the plumage somewhat duller.

Length 4.60, wing 2.76, tail 1.95, tarsus .68, bill .56.

The present species is included on the authority of Mr. N. B. Moore, who claims to have seen five or six of these Warblers during the months of November, December, and January, while at Nassau.

Fig. Aud. Bds. N. A., Vol. II. pl. 105.

DENDRŒCA ÆSTIVA. (Gm.)
SUMMER WARBLER.

Adult Male. — Tarsus less than .65 *of an inch;* general plumage, bright yellow; breast and sides of the body streaked with rufous;

tail, yellow, having the outer webs and tips brownish; wing-coverts edged with yellow.

Adult Female. — Much paler, and showing the rufous streaks very faintly, if at all.

Length 5.15, wing 2.66, tail 2.25, tarsus .64.

I include this species on the authority of Dr. Bryant, as I have never met with the true *D. æstiva* in the Bahamas.

Fig. Aud. Bds. N. A., Vol. II. pl. 88.

DENDRŒCA PETECHIA. (*Linn*)

Tarsus not less than .70 of an inch; outer webs of tail-feathers showing dusky.

Adult Male. — General appearance of the last species; nape showing olive; sides streaked; crown, greenish, and sometimes tinged with rufous anteriorly.

This Warbler was not uncommon at Inagua and Long Island during May and June; none were seen during the winter. Dr. Bryant found it at Inagua, where he says it was quite abundant, both among the mangroves and in the clumps of trees on the savanna.

DENDRŒCA PETECHIA VAR. GUNDLACHI. (*Linn.*) (*Baird.*)
Gundlach's Warbler.

Adult Male. — *Lower part of throat streaked;* above, yellowish green; crown showing no signs of rufous, or only a faint tinge; tarsus, about .82. Sometimes difficult to distinguish plumage from that of the preceding species.

The present variety becomes quite abundant during the summer months. In its habits, it resembles *D. æstiva*, to which it is very closely allied. None were observed north of Long Island.

DENDRŒCA CÆRULESCENS. (*Linn.*)
Black-throated Blue Warbler.

Adult Male. — Above, slaty blue; sides of the head, throat, and sides of the body, black; rest of under parts, white; a band of white on the primaries; tail, dark brown, blotched with white.

Adult Female. — Smaller than the male; above, olive-green, reaching the sides of the throat; under parts, pale greenish yellow.

Length 5, wing 2.40, tail .90, tarsus .72, bill .36.

The Black-throated Blue Warbler can only be considered as a rather rare winter visitant. On May 8, an adult male, evidently migrating, came on board the vessel near Isac Key. None were observed later. It generally frequents the pine woods, such as are found on the islands of New Providence and Abaco.

Fig. Aud. Bds. N. A., Vol. II. pl. 95.

DENDRŒCA CORONATA. (*Linn.*)
YELLOW-RUMPLED WARBLER.

Winter Plumage, Male. — Above, brown, faintly streaked with black; under parts, yellowish white, streaked with dark brown upon the sides and breast; *rump* and *crown, yellow*, the latter almost concealed by the brown tips of the feathers; two distinct wing-bands, and spots on the three outer tail-feathers, white. Female, in winter, differs but slightly from the male.

Length 5.40, wing 2.80, tail 2.20, tarsus .70, bill .40.

A rather common visitant. We found them numerous in the vicinity of Nassau, N. P., during the months of December and January, and occasionally observed them on some of the other islands. It is a tame, pretty little species, generally frequenting the heavy growth, and may be easily recognized by the yellow on the rump.

Fig. Aud. Bds. N. A., Vol. II. pl. 76.

DENDRŒCA BLACKBURNIÆ. (Gm.)
BLACKBURNIAN WARBLER.

Adult Male. — Above, black; a white scapular stripe middle of the crown; side of head and neck, throat, to the upper breast, bright orange-red; under parts, white, showing orange on the belly, and streaked with black on the sides; tail, brown; outer tail-feathers, white, tipped with brown; wing-coverts showing much white.

Adult Female. — Resembles the male; breast is much paler. In winter, males become pale, and show large stripes of black on the sides.

Length 4.52, wing 2.60, tail 2, tarsus .68, bill .40.

Nothing is known concerning the occurrence of the Blackburnian Warbler in the Bahama Islands, except a short note by Dr. Bryant, in which he states that he saw a pair on April 30.

On one occasion, while shooting in the woods near Nassau, I saw what I believed to be a bird of this species; but upon shooting it, it proved to be only a highly colored specimen of *D. dominica.* If Dr. Bryant was not mistaken in the species, it is probably of rare occurrence in the Bahamas.

Fig. Aud. Bds. N. A., Vol. II. pl. 87.

DENDRŒCA STRIATA. (*Forst.*)

BLACK-POLL WARBLER.

Adult Male.—Above, grayish, tinged with brown and streaked with black; top of the head and nape, black; under parts, throat, lower sides of the head, and ear-coverts, white; sides of the throat and body streaked with black; two white bars on the wing-coverts; wings and tail, brownish; tail-feathers showing white on the inner webs.

Adult Female.—Upper parts, greenish, streaked with dark brown; under parts tinged with yellowish.

Length 5, wing 3, tail 2.16, tarsus .80, bill .40.

I cannot speak of this bird from personal observation, as I never met with it in the Bahamas. Dr. Bryant, however, found it abundant from the 1st to the 10th of May, and says, " In its habits, this bird approximates very nearly to the *M. varia*, climbing round the trunks of trees in search of insects apparently with the same facility as the latter bird."

Fig. Aud. Bds. N. A., Vol. II. pl. 78.

DENDRŒCA PENNSYLVANICA. (*Linn.*)
CHESTNUT-SIDED WARBLER.

Adult Male. — Above, striped with black and gray, becoming olive and black on the lower back; crown, yellow, bordered by a black stripe; cheeks, black, continuing in a narrow stripe to the chestnut of the sides; under parts, white; sides, bright chestnut; inner web of the outer tail-feathers showing white.

Adult Female. — Like the male, but paler; much less chestnut; the black on the cheeks wanting, or replaced by a dull brown.

Length 4.80, wing 2.75, tail 2.05, tarsus .72, bill .40.

I have included this Warbler on the authority of Dr. Bryant, who says that he saw a few in the early part of May.

Fig. Aud. Bds. N. A., Vol. II. pl. 81.

DENDRŒCA MACULOSA. (*Gm.*)
BLACK AND YELLOW WARBLER.

Adult Male. — Above, black; crown, gray, edged with white behind the eye, a band of black passing from the bill through the eye to the neck; under parts, yellow, streaked with black; crissum, white; rump, showing yellow, wing-coverts forming a white patch; tail, black, having a band of white at the middle.

Adult Female. — Resembles the male, but is duller in coloration ; the black on the head merely a triangular patch.

Length 4.70, wing 2.40, tail 1.96, tarsus .64, bill .28.

Dr. Bryant includes this Warbler in his list, and considers it as abundant as it is in the United States. I have included it on his authority.

Fig. Aud. Bds. N. A., Vol. II. pl. 96.

DENDRŒCA TIGRINA. (Gm.)
CAPE MAY WARBLER.

Winter Plumage, Male. — Upper parts, olive-green, slightly marked with black ; feathers of the head, black, edged with gray, giving the top of the head a mottled appearance ; ear-coverts showing very slight tinge of chestnut ; superciliary stripe, yellow ; a yellow band passing round the sides of the throat, nearly joining above ; under parts, bright yellow, streaked with black ; quills and tail, dark brown, edged with yellowish white ; three outer tail-feathers with patch of white upon the inner webs ; rump, yellow ; crissum yellowish white.

Winter Plumage, Female. — Above, olivaceous ash, showing yellowish on the rump ; no black or chestnut about the head ; tail-spots not so clear as in the male ; beneath, whitish, slightly tinged with yellow on the breast, and streaked with dusky, not black, as in the male.

Length 4.75, wing 2.80, tail 2, tarsus .80, bill .40.

The present species, although not abundant, is found throughout the Bahamas during the winter. We occasionally met with it during December and January, and on the 26th of the latter month I observed several of them flitting about among the trees in front of the hotel at Nassau. Its food, like others of its family, consists mainly of insects.

Fig. Aud. Bds. N. A., Vol. II. pl. 85.

DENDRŒCA DISCOLOR. (*Vieil.*)
PRAIRIE WARBLER.

Winter Plumage, Male. — Above, olive-green; the interscapular region with faint indications of chestnut; under parts, yellow, faintly striped with ash upon the sides; throat, yellow, showing slight traces of white; a narrow yellow stripe from the nostril encircling the eye, broken at its posterior part by a streak of ash; quills and tail-feathers, brown, edged with white; two outer tail-feathers with a long patch of white upon the inner webs.

Winter Plumage, Female. — Similar to the male, but the markings much paler; yellow stripe of the eye very indistinct, and of a pale yellowish white.

Length 4.50, wing 2.10, tail 2, tarsus .74, bill .40.

This pretty little Warbler is one of the most abundant species found on the islands. Upon almost every key, large enough to admit of the growth of a few bushes, they were to be found, searching diligently for their food, and twittering cheerfully to one another, without seeming to mind my presence in the least. Dr. Bryant states that he thought this species a constant resident in the Bahamas, and that it breeds there, as after the middle of April he saw none that were not mated. It is possible that a few individuals may remain through the summer, but there can be no doubt that most if not all of them leave the islands before the last of April. I did not meet with it after May 1.

Fig. Aud. Bds. N. A., Vol. II. pl. 97.

DENDRŒCA DOMINICA. (*Linn.*)
Yellow-throated Warbler.

Winter Plumage, Male. — Above, grayish blue; forehead, lores, cheeks, and sides of the throat, and streaks on the sides of the breast, black; superciliary line, white, with a yellowish tinge at the base of the bill; small white line under the eye; sides of the neck behind the cheek-patch, and two bands on the wings, white; throat and part of breast, bright yellow; lower part of breast and belly, white, the latter with broad black stripes upon the sides; the outer webs of the three outer tail-feathers patched with white. Female slightly smaller and paler, showing a trace of brown upon the belly.

Length 5.15, wing 2.60, tail 2.20, tarsus .65, bill .50.

The Yellow-throated Warbler is a rather common winter visitant, frequenting the tall trees, generally the pines. At Nassau it was quite abundant in the "pine barrens." Its food consists principally of small insects and larvæ. It is possible that some few of these birds remain in the Bahamas to breed, although none were observed during the summer season. The nest of this species is exceeding rare, and only on one occasion have I had the good fortune to find it breeding. The nest was taken April 28, near Jacksonville, Fla. It was built in the middle of a clump of Spanish moss, suspended from the end of a large branch about twenty feet from the ground, and contained four eggs, which were quite fresh. The egg is of a dull, bluish-white color, thickly dotted with fine brown spots around the larger end.

Fig. Aud. Bds. N. A., Vol. II. pl. 79.

DENDRŒCA KIRTLANDI. *Baird.*

KIRTLAND'S WARBLER.

Winter Plumage, Female. — Above, bluish ash ; the feathers of the crown with a narrow, those of the middle of the back with a broad streak of dark brown; a narrow semicircular ring of black surrounds the eye, touching its anterior part; eyelids, white; under parts, yellow; throat and breast with small spots, and sides of the body with short streaks of black ; greater and middle wing-coverts, primaries, and tail-feathers edged with dull white; two outer tail-feathers with a dull white spot on the inner web; under tail-coverts, yellowish white. The sexes are similar.

Length 5.50, wing 2.75, tail 2.50, tarsus .80.

This rare species may be considered a winter visitant to the Bahamas. On Jan. 9 a specimen was taken at Hawk's Nest, on Andros Island, which proved to be a female. Its actions much resembled those of *D. coronata*, and it seemed to prefer keeping among the thick brush to the more open ground. Its stomach contained the remains of insects.

Mr. H. A. Purdie, of Newton, Mass., in his notes regarding this Warbler, gives the following list of specimens now known to science:— *

" 1. Male, caught on a vessel at sea off Abaco, Bahamas, by Dr. Samuel Cabot, of Boston, the second week in October, 1841. Not identified until some years after the type specimen was described.

" 2. Male, taken by Dr. J. P. Kirtland, near Cleveland, O., May 13, 1851. Type of species.

" 3. Female, obtained by R. K. Winslow, near Cleveland, O., in June, 1860.

" 4. Male, shot by Charles Dury, at Cincinnati, O., the first week in May, 1872.

* Bulletin of the Nuttall Ornithological Club, Vol. IV. p. 185.

"5. Female, collected by A. B. Covert, at Ann Arbor, Mich., May 15, 1875.

"6 and 7. Male and female, taken by Messrs. William and John Hall, at Rockport, Cuyahoga County, O., May, 1878.

"8. Female, collected by Charles B. Cory, on Andros Island, Bahamas, Jan. 9, 1879.

"9. Female, taken by A. B. Covert, Ann Arbor, Mich., May 16, 1879."

DENDRŒCA PALMARUM. (Gm.)

YELLOW RED-POLL WARBLER.

Winter Plumage, Male. — Above, olive-brown, the feathers with darker centres, becoming olive-green upon the rump; crown of the head showing indistinct trace of chestnut; throat and superciliary line from nostril, pale yellowish white; under parts, yellowish white, becoming brighter upon the belly, streaked with pale brown; crissum, pale yellow; outer edges of wing and tail-feathers, yellowish white; a white patch at the end of the inner webs of the two outer tail-feathers.

Winter Plumage, Female. — Slightly smaller than the male; chestnut entirely wanting upon the crown; throat more of a brownish cast, and general plumage slightly darker.

Length 4.85, wing 2.45, tail 2.20, tarsus .78, bill .40.

This pretty little Warbler is very abundant during the winter months. Dr. Bryant states, in "Proceedings Boston Society Natural History," Vol. IX., "During the winter and early spring this bird was extremely abundant, but confined almost entirely to the neighborhood of the sea-coast. Its habits are decidedly terrestrial, and it approaches, in this respect, very nearly to the Titlarks. They were constantly running along the edge of the road, or else hopping among the low shrubs in the pastures. I did not see a single individual seeking for food amidst the large trees, although we found it abundant everywhere."

I obtained most of my specimens among the pines in the interior of the island. By April 15 all had left, and very few remain until that date.

Fig. Aud. Bds. N. A., Vol. II. pl. 90.

DENDRŒCA PINUS. (Wils.)
PINE-CREEPING WARBLER.

Winter Plumage, Male. — Above, olive-green; a yellow superciliary line from the base of the bill; under parts, with the exception of the belly, bright yellow; the sides of the breast with indistinct streaks of olive; sides of the head, olive-green; belly and crissum, dusky white; wings and tail, dark brown, the feathers edged with dusky white, the former showing two distinct bands; inner webs of the two outer tail-feathers showing oblique patches of dull white.

Winter Plumage, Female.—Smaller than the male, and much paler; upper parts, grayish, with trace of olive; throat, very pale yellow, becoming grayish brown upon the sides of the belly; side of the head and neck, gray.

Length 5.50, wing 2.80, tail 2.35, tarsus .80, bill .50.

The Pine-creeping Warbler is a winter visitant, and one of the most abundant species of its family. During the month of January they were to be seen everywhere among the pine woods, running along the trunks of trees after the manner of the Creepers. Their food appears to be almost entirely insectivorous. Although so abundant at the present time, Dr. Bryant procured but one specimen during his visit to the Bahamas. Some few birds remain throughout the year, and probably breed. We procured specimens as late as June 19, and observed several after that date.

Fig. Aud. Bds. N. A., Vol. II. pl. 82.

SEIURUS AUROCAPILLUS. (*Linn.*)
GOLDEN-CROWNED THRUSH.

Local Name.— Night Walker.

Winter Plumage, Male.— Above, olive-green; crown, brownish orange, bordered by two black streaks from base of the bill to nape; under parts, white, with an olive tint upon the sides; breast and sides of the belly streaked with dark brown; crissum, white; legs, pale flesh-color. The female does not differ from the male.

Length 5.80, wing 3.05, tail 2.30, tarsus .90, bill .58.

The Golden-crowned Thrush is not uncommon throughout the islands during the winter months, seeming to prefer the thick undergrowth to the more open portions of the country. Dr. Bryant found it common at Nassau in 1866. None remain later than April. Its food consists principally of insects.

Fig. Aud. Bds. N. A., Vol. III. pl. 148.

SEIURUS NOVEBORACENSIS. (Gm.)
WATER THRUSH.

Local Name. — Night Walker.

Winter Plumage, Male. — Above, olive-brown, with a slight shade of green; a superciliary line from the bill to the nape; pale yellow, showing faint indications of brown; a band of pale brown passes through the eye from bill to nape; under parts, pale yellow; breast and sides heavily streaked, and throat finely spotted with dark brown; wings and tail, olive-brown. The female resembles the male.

Length 5.50, wing 2.80, tail 2.20, tarsus .80, bill .50.

This, as well as the preceding species, is called Night Walker by the inhabitants. It frequents damp ground, seeming to prefer that which is surrounded by an almost impenetrable undergrowth.

I procured but three specimens, although it cannot be considered at all rare, and is a regular winter visitant. Dr. Bryant found it common throughout the islands in 1866. It is rarely seen, on account of its retiring habits.

Fig. Aud. Bds. N. A., Vol. III. pl. 149.

GEOTHLYPIS TRICHAS. (*Linn.*)
MARYLAND YELLOW-THROATED WARBLER.

Winter Plumage, Male. — Upper parts, olive-green; throat, bright yellow, becoming greenish upon the belly, and olive upon the sides; *a broad black line passing from the sides of the neck through the eye and over the forehead*, with a suffusion of gray behind it upon the crown, and faintly visible along its upper edge; crissum, pale yellow; wings and tail, olive-green, the former showing a yellow line upon the carpus. Some birds show a slight tinge of brown upon the head.

Winter Plumage, Female. — Pale olive above and yellowish below. No black on the head.

Length 4.60, wing 2.20, tail 2.25, tarsus .80, bill .40.

This well-known and beautiful Ground Warbler is common throughout the larger islands of the Bahamas. Its habits are the same as when it enlivens the hedges with us during the summer months. Dr. Bryant states, " While lying at anchor, on the 20th of

April, in the harbor of Grassy Creek, a flock of these birds commenced flying by the vessel, and continued without intermission for two hours. They did not fly in a compact body, but were constantly passing during this time, more or less being in sight the whole period. Many of them alighted on the vessel All of them that I saw were males. On the 10th of May, they were still abundant in the neighborhood of Nassau."

This species frequents the low, thick brush, and keeps so well concealed that it is rarely seen, although in reality it is quite as abundant as many other species which appear much more common.

Fig. Aud. Bds. N. A., Vol. II. pl. 102.

GEOTHLYPIS ROSTRATUS. *Bryant.*
Greater Yellow-throated Warbler.

Winter Plumage, Male. — Above, bright olive-green, a broad band of black passing from the sides of the neck over the forehead, including the eye, and extending to the nostril, just touching the lower mandible, the black bordered posteriorly with pearl-gray, becoming deeper gray upon the crown; under parts, bright yellow, the flanks shaded with olive; quills, brown, with the outer webs olive-green, third primary longest.

Winter Plumage, Female. — The black band wanting; plumage slightly paler; a pale ash-colored line from over the eye to sides of the neck; crown showing a trace of brown, otherwise resembles the male.

Length 5.50, wing 2.70, tail 2.36, tarsus .92, bill .72.

The present species appears to be an exceedingly local and rare bird, all the known specimens having been taken upon the island of New Providence. During my visits to that island I had the good fortune to procure a female, which has been hitherto undescribed. Its habits appeared to be much the same as those of *G. trichas*, with the exception that it seemed to prefer somewhat higher and dryer ground than the latter species. Dr. Bryant states, "The stomach and œsophagus of one contained the head and body of an Anolis, which, without the tail, measured ten inches and a half in length, showing rather a carnivorous propensity for a bird of this family."

It is easily distinguished from *G. trichas* by its great size, and the absence of white upon the abdomen. I give below the comparative measurement of a large specimen of *G. trichas* and *G. rostratus*, both taken in the same locality.

	Length.	Wing.	Tail.	Tarsus.	Bill.
G. trichas,	4.50	2.20	2.25	.80	.40
G. rostratus,	5.50	2.70	2.36	.92	.72

Of late years this bird has been classed as a large local variety of *G. trichas;* but, after a careful comparison of several specimens with a large series of the latter, I have, without hesitation, restored it to the rank of a distinct species.

SETOPHAGA RUTICILLA. (*Linn.*)
REDSTART.

Winter Plumage, Male. — Upper parts and throat, black; belly, white, slightly tinged with orange; wings, black, *with a broad band of orange;* basal half of the tail-feathers, except the middle ones, and a patch on each side of the breast, orange-red.

Winter Plumage, Female. — Black replaced by olive-green; an ashy appearance upon the head; the orange-red replaced by pale yellow.

Length 5.20, wing 2.45, tail 2.38, tarsus .70, bill .18.

The Redstart appeared to be quite abundant during the winter upon the larger islands. A few were seen in the latter part of December, and later it became common. It is easily recognized by the red appearance of the wings as it darts in and out of the undergrowth in search of insects. Merely a winter resident, it does not remain to breed, and rarely remains until May, although Dr. Bryant states that he found it abundant until May 13.

Fig. Aud. Bds. N. A., Vol. I. pl. 68.

FAM. CŒREBIDÆ.

CREEPERS.

CERTHIOLA BAHAMENSIS. Reich.
BAHAMA HONEY CREEPER.

Local Name.— Banana Bird.

Winter Plumage, Male.— Above, black, with a slight grayish tinge; a slight superciliary line from bill to nape; throat, ashy white; breast, bright yellow, extending upon the sides of the abdomen, and shading into gray upon the flanks; crissum, white; wing-feathers slightly edged with dull white; a white patch at the base of the primaries, forming a bar on the wings; edge of the carpus bright yellow; tail, color of the back, tipped with white, wanting upon the middle, and largest upon the two outer feathers.

Adult Female.— Slightly paler than the male, but otherwise resembling it.

Length 4.50, wing 2.60, tail 1.90, tarsus .70, bill .54.

This pretty little Creeper is one of the most abundant species inhabiting the Bahamas. We found it upon every island that we visited. Its food seemed to consist of insects and the honey which it extracts from the flowers. The stomachs of several specimens which I examined contained nothing but insects.

Regarding the food of this bird, Dr. Bryant states. "On my arrival at Nassau the leaf of life (*Verea crenata*) was in full bloom, and these birds seemed to derive their whole subsistence from the insects found in the flowers. These it did not procure by inserting its bill into the flower, but by thrusting it through the petals. After the flowers had disappeared, I saw them in large numbers about the sour oranges, devouring the juice and pulp of the fruit, and also the small insects attracted there."

Mr. N. B. Moore states, "There is much delicious nectar within the flower of this plant (*Verea crenata*), of which the *Certhiola* is very fond, and which it has learned to obtain by thrusting its bill through the petals. I have spent much time in examining these flowers, and never, but in one instance, and that of a malformed one, did I find an insect in the nectary until it had been penetrated by the bill of the bird. After an opening had been made by him, very small black ants and very small winged insects may be found therein."

The period of incubation commences during the latter part of March.

FAM. HIRUNDINIDÆ.

SWALLOWS.

HIRUNDO HORREORUM. Barton.

BARN SWALLOW.

Adult Male. — Above, lustrous blue; under parts, pale chestnut; forehead and throat much darker; breast showing an imperfect blue band; tail forked, all but the two central feathers showing white on the inner web. Female similar.

Length 6.80, wing 4.90, tail 4.45.

Dr. Bryant states, in his "Additions to a List of Birds seen at the Bahamas," "According to Mr. Sargent, a very large flock of these birds visited the island (Inagua) some years since, and remained several days. He had never seen the Bahama Swallow there." I have included the present species on this authority, but something more definite should be learned concerning it before it can hold a place in the ari-fauna of the Bahamas.

Fig. Aud. Bds. N. A., Vol. I. pl. 48.

HIRUNDO CYANEOVIRIDIS. (*Bryant.*)

BAHAMA SWALLOW.

Adult Male. — Above, velvet green, shading into steel-blue, with purple reflections upon the rump and wings; a black stripe from the nostrils to the eye; under parts, pure white; tail forked, the inner webs of the outer feathers edged with dull white.

Adult Female. — Resembles the male, but the plumage much duller, and showing traces of dusky; bill and feet black.

Length 6.40, wing 4.40, tail 3.10, tarsus .42, bill .15.

The beautiful little Bahama Swallow seems to be restricted to the Bahama Islands. A few were seen on Andros Island in January, but they were flying high, and we were unable to shoot them. During the month of June they became very abundant in the neighborhood of Nassau, and I was enabled to procure a fine series of specimens. In their habits they do not seem to differ from our common species (*T. bicolor*), except perhaps that they are not as quick in their movements. Their food seems to be entirely insectivorous.

Dr. Bryant says, regarding this species, " In the style of its coloring, it resembles more nearly *H. thalassina* than any other species. I have no doubt that it has been confounded by European naturalists with *H. bicolor*, though its resemblance to this species is very slight. I saw them during the whole of my stay at Nassau, but only on the first mile of the road leading to the west of the island. They were so abundant there that thirty or forty could be seen at almost all times." He also says, " They generally followed the road up and down, seldom flying high, but skimming along near the ground. I did not succeed in finding their nests, and could not ascertain whether they bred on the island or not. I killed no specimens after the 28th of April. Up to this date, the genital organs exhibited no appearance of excitement. The stomachs of those dissected contained almost entirely small *dipterous* insects, some of them extremely minute."

TACHYCINETA BICOLOR. (*Vieil.*)
WHITE-BELLIED SWALLOW.

Adult Male. — Above, lustrous *steel-blue;* under parts, pure white. Female much duller in plumage.

Length 6, wing 5, tail 2.40.

I have included this Swallow on the authority of Mr. L. J. K. Brace, of Nassau, who says, " During the stormy weather of Dec. 1 and 2 of last year, a number of these birds were to be seen flying about. On the 1st, I saw only three, but on the 2d a great many, which flew very low, close to the ground; two flew inside the house, and clung for a few minutes to the edge of a shelf, but before they could be secured, flew out again. On the 4th, the weather moderating, not one was to be seen."

It is exceedingly unfortunate that a specimen was not killed, as the resemblance, even at a short distance, of the Bahama Swallow to the present species is so close as to render identification difficult, and the capture of a specimen would have removed all doubt of its identity.

Fig. Aud. Bds. N. A., Vol. I. pl. 46.

FAM. VIREONIDÆ.

VIREOS.

VIREO ALTILOQUUS VAR. BARBATULUS. (*Vieil.*) (*Cab.*)

BLACK-WHISKERED VIREO.

Adult Male. — Crown, slaty-gray; upper parts, olive-green; a dull white superciliary line, and a dusky stripe through the eye; a narrow brownish maxillary line on the sides of the chin; sides, olive; under parts, white; crissum, yellow; iris, red.

Length 5.80, wing 3, tail 2.40, tarsus .66, bill .52.

My first specimen of the Vireo was taken May 11, but it probably arrives in the Bahamas somewhat earlier. Dr. Bryant states that he found it very abundant, arriving about the 1st of May. "The note of this bird did not appear to me to resemble the syllables *Whip-tom-kelly* more than any others, although this might be introduced as part of the note, pronouncing the first syllable very distinctly, and terminating with an additional note longer than any; thus, Whip-tom-kelly pheuu, and frequently still another long note." I am unable to state anything, from personal observation, regarding its breeding habits.

VIREO FLAVIFRONS. Vieil.

YELLOW-THROATED VIREO.

Adult Male. — Above, olive-green; a superciliary line and a ring around the eye, yellow; throat and breast, yellow; belly and crissum, white; wings, olive-gray, with two white bands; tail-feathers edged with white; bill and legs, bluish.

Length 5.75, wing 2.90, tail 2.20.

I have never met with this species in the Bahamas, but have included it on the authority of Mr. N. B. Moore, who states that he saw two birds of this species feeding upon the berries of the gumbo-limbo-tree, in company with *V. crassirostris.*

Fig. Aud. Bds. N. A., Vol. IV. pl. 238.

LANIVIREO CRASSIROSTRIS. (Bryant)

COMMON VIREO.

Winter Plumage, Male. — Above, yellowish olive, a streak of yellow from the nostril encircling the eye; under parts, yellowish; wings and tail, brown, the feathers edged with greenish, the former showing two white bands.

Length 5, wing 2.40, tail 1.90, tarsus .84, bill .40.

This little Vireo is very abundant throughout the islands. I found it especially common in the neighborhood of Nassau. Dr. Bryant considered it quite rare, as he says, " This species of Vireo is, I think, undescribed. It is not a common bird; three specimens were all I obtained. When first seen, I mistook it for the White-eyed Vireo. I noticed nothing remarkable in its habits. All the specimens procured were actively engaged in hunting insects in small trees in the midst of a clearing, about three miles from the city, on the road leading to the south side of the island. The first specimen was procured in March, the other two, a pair, in May."

It is a resident, and breeds in June; but I was unable to find the nest, although during the latter part of the month I observed several birds which evidently had young. The stomachs of several specimens which I dissected contained the remains of berries and insects.

FAM. FRINGILLIDÆ.

FINCHES.

LOXIGILLA VIOLACEA. (*Linn.*)
PURPLE GROSBEAK.

Local Name. — Spanish Paroquet.

Winter Plumage, Male. — Entire plumage black, showing a slight brownish tinge upon the quills, throat, crissum, and a crescent over the eye, reddish brown; bill and legs, black.

Winter Plumage, Female. — Upper parts, gray, with a tinge of olive-green upon the back; below, ash, lightest upon the belly, showing a tinge of olive upon the breast and sides; quills with fine edgings of dull white; crissum, a crescent over the eye, and markings upon the chin, pale reddish brown, much lighter than in the male; under mandible pale. Immature birds resemble the female.

Length 6, wing 3, tail 2.85, tarsus, .80, bill .50.

The Purple Grosbeak, or Spanish Paroquet as it is called by the negroes, is abundant throughout the Bahama Islands. Upon every island of any size which we visited, the thick undergrowth resounded with its peculiar notes. It is very retiring in its habits, rarely being seen in the open. The inhabitants claim that it destroys great quantities of fruit, but I cannot answer for the truth of this statement, as the stomachs of all those dissected by me contained only insects and berries, and I have never seen it eating fruit of any kind.

As I never had the good fortune of finding the nest of this species, I quote from Mr. Gosse, who says, "One of those gigantic and hoary cotton-trees, which are the pride of a Jamaica forest, or some other tree equally tall, is usually selected by this Bullfinch for its abode. At the extremity of an immense horizontal limb, it builds a nest of rude materials, as large as a half-bushel measure, the opening being near the bottom. I have seen the bird enter this monstrous structure, but have had no opportunity of examining it. Dr. Robinson observes that 'the Black Bullfinch builds a nest as big as a Blackbird's cage, and, by the artful contrivance of this little volatile, the whole has the simple appearance of a heap of trash, flung on some bough of a tree, as it were, by accident, so that nobody would suppose it to be anything else.' And in another passage, he records having found the nest at Negril, on the 22d of April, 1761, at the summit of a cabbage-palm, eighty-one feet high, which he caused to be felled. 'Among the spadices of this tree was fixed, how, I cannot tell, the nest of the Black Bullfinch, made up of various matter, viz., old cane-trash fibres, silk-cotton, some dry leaves, and at the bottom many tendrils of climbing shrubs, and a very small species of *epidendrum*, or green wyth, common in this parish. In it I found one egg about an inch long, in color like that of a common Duck, that is, of a sullied white.'"

I have followed the older authors in calling this bird the Purple Grosbeak, but I do not think the name a good one, as I have never seen a specimen which showed the least signs of purple, although several in my collection have a faint greenish tinge on the back.

This is the *Coccothraustes purpurea* of Catesby.

LOXIGILLA NOCTIS. (Linn.)
BLACK GROSBEAK.

Local Name. — Black Charles.

Adult Male. — General plumage, black; a narrow superciliary stripe, chin-patch (reaching the sides of the throat), and crissum, brownish red; bill and legs, black.

Adult Female. — Resembling the female *L. violacea*, somewhat smaller. Immature birds often show much gray.

Length 5.25, wing 2.75, tail 2.20, tarsus .60, bill .40.

The present species was quite common in Inagua during the months of May and June, but whether it is a resident, or simply a summer visitant from some of the more southern islands, I am unable to say. Its habits, as far as I was able to observe, appeared to be the same as those of *L. violacea*, to which it is very closely allied.

PASSERCULUS SAVANNA. (*Wils.*)
Savanna Sparrow.

Adult Male. — General plumage streaked with blackish and bay; below, buff, streaked with dusky and brown; edge of the wings and superciliary line, yellowish.

Length 5.30, wing 2.60, tail 2.20.

I include this species provisionally, never having taken it in the Bahamas. One Sunday afternoon in January, while walking through a field at Long Bay Key, Andros Island, I observed a number of small Sparrows flitting about in the grass. Unfortunately, I had no gun, but approaching them as near as they would allow, I made them out to be *P. savanna*. I never met with it afterwards, but there is no reason why it should not visit these islands, as it has been recorded from Cuba.

Fig. Aud. Bds. N. A., Vol. III. pl. 160.

PASSER DOMESTICUS. Linn.
English Sparrow.

Adult Male. — Above, grayish brown; upper part of the back streaked with black, tawny, and rufous; a patch of chestnut on the side of the head; cheeks and side of the throat, dull white; crown, gray; throat and upper part of the breast, black, some of the lower feathers edged with gray; below, brownish white; wing-coverts, chestnut and black, crossed and tipped with dull white, forming two wing-bands; tail, brown; bill, black.

Adult Female. — Colors of the male, replaced by light and dark brown; olive-brown on the head; under parts, brownish white; wing-bands indistinct.

Length 5.10, wing 2.84, tail 2.36, tarsus .68, bill .36.

Mr. L. J. K. Brace states that the English Sparrow has been introduced into the Bahamas within the last few years, and I was told by several gentlemen that it still exists there; but during my different visits to the islands I have never met with it.

CYANOSPIZA CIRIS. (*Linn.*)
NONPAREIL.

Adult Male. — Head, blue; back, green; rump, brownish red; under parts, red, becoming pale on the belly; tail, reddish brown; upper mandible, black; lower mandible, pale.

Adult Female. — Above, green, showing slight golden reflections on the back; under parts, pale yellow, greenish on the breast; slightly smaller than the male.

Length 4.80, wing 2.60, tail 2, tarsus .80, bill .40.

Mr. N. B. Moore includes this species in his list, stating that he saw a male in splendid dress on February 9. It may occasionally visit the islands, but cannot be considered as a regular visitant.

Fig. Aud. Bds. N. A.. Vol. III. pl. 169.

CYANOSPIZA CYANEA. (*Linn.*)

INDIGO BIRD.

Adult Male.— General color, blue, deep on the crown and throat; wing brown, and tail brown, touched with blue; bill, dark brown.

Adult Female.— General plumage, reddish brown; paler and somewhat mottled below, becoming whitish on the belly.

Length 4.60, wing 2.60, tail 2.10, tarsus .65, bill .37.

Mr. N. B. Moore states that while at Nassau he saw a male November 1, and a "female, or young male, November 1 and November 13." I have given it a place among the birds of the Bahamas upon his authority.

Fig. Aud. Bds. N. A., Vol. III. pl. 170.

PHONIPARA BICOLOR. (*Linn.*)
BLACK-FACED FINCH.

Local Names. — Paroquet and Banana Bird.

Winter Plumage, Male. — Above, olive-green, shading into black on the crown; cheeks and under parts totally black in the adult, and ranging from this to a black throat and greenish white belly in immature birds; wings and tail, color of the back; upper mandible, dark; lower mandible, pale.

Winter Plumage, Female. — Above, olive-green, lighter than the male; under parts, ashy, with a slight tinge of olive; otherwise, like the male.

Length 4.30, wing 2.05, tail 1.85, tarsus .70, bill .37.

This little Finch is abundant everywhere, and is very domestic in its habits. It seems to prefer living near the habitation of man, as it becomes far less common in uninhabited districts. The males differ greatly in plumage, some of them having the entire under parts black, while others have simply a black throat. I think the former represents the full plumage of an adult bird. Their note is a short, sharp "chip," uttered while perched or fluttering among the bushes. Its food consists of insects, berries, and often fruit of various kinds.

This is the *Passerculus bicolor bahamensis* of Catesby.

SPINDALIS ZENA. (Linn.)

BAHAMA FINCH.

Winter Plumage, Male.—Above, black; rump and a broad band over the nape from side of the neck, rufous brown, shading into an orange tinge; a superciliary stripe, and a stripe on the sides of the throat from lower mandible and chin, white; cheeks, black; throat, black, shading into brown upon the breast, with a yellow stripe passing from the chin nearly to the brown of the breast; breast, deep yellow, shading into brown as it nears the throat; belly, white, with an olive tint upon the flanks; wings and tail black, edged with white; the tertials, coverts, and base of primaries heavily marked with white; bill, black under mandible, bluish; legs, black.

Winter Plumage, Female. — Above, olive-green; below, paler, shading into white on the belly; the sides and flanks, pale olive-green; the stripe over the eye but faintly indicated, and of an ashy color; wings and tail, dark brown, with an olive tinge on the feathers, showing markings of dull white as in the male, but much narrower.

Length 5.95, wing 3, tail 2.50, tarsus .80, bill .50.

This beautiful species is a resident of the Bahamas. We found it most abundant on the island of New Providence, where it is one of the first birds that attracts the visitor's attention on account of its

brilliant coloration. Dr. Bryant states that its food consists almost
entirely of small berries, and, according to my observation, this statement is correct; but they also eat many species of insects, and
sometimes fruits. Although very abundant near Nassau, on the
island of New Providence, they are rather uncommon at Long
Island, and only a single specimen was seen at Inagua. Gosse
found this species near Spanish Town, Jamaica, where he claims
it was not common. He gives an interesting account of a bird of
this species which he procured alive. He says: —

"I carried him home in my handkerchief, and put him into a
large cage, where he soon became quite a favorite. From the very
first, he was fearless and lively, found the use of the perches immediately, and did not flutter or beat himself against the sides, though
persons stood close to the cage. This was large enough to allow a
short flight, and as there were several perches inserted at various
heights and distances into the sides, he spent a great deal of his
time in leaping from one to the other, seeming to enjoy it much.
Seeing this, I put in one or two more, which were no sooner ready
than he took notice of them; cautiously, at first, as if doubtful
whether they could bear him. Soon, however, he ventured boldly,
and then took them regularly in his course. He always slept on
the highest perch, with his head behind his wing. He was in full
plumage, and his gay breast and the fine contrasts of his striped
head and wings showed him off to advantage. I knew nothing that
he would eat, save the berries of the bully-tree, none of which grew
within a considerable distance. I first tried him with a few insects

and small earthworms, but he took no notice of these; then I gathered a few bunches of fiddlewood berries, which I had no sooner stuck into his cage than I was pleased to see him hop towards them and pick off the ripe ones with much relish and discrimination. I was informed, in a wild state, he sometimes eats the sour-sop. As I had none of this fruit at hand, I gave him pieces of a ripe custard-apple and of a guava. He immediately began to eat of each, plucking off portions of the pulp, and also taking up the fleshy ovaria of which the former is composed, which he chewed with his beak till the inclosed seed was pressed out.

"But all these were forsaken so soon as I presented to him bunches of ripe pimento, black and sweet. These he picked off greedily, masticating each in the beak, until the seeds, which I suppose were too hotly aromatic for his taste, fell out. It was amusing to see the persevering efforts he made to obtain those berries which happened to be a little beyond his reach He would jump from perch to perch impatiently, gazing with outstretched neck at the tempting fruit, then jump and look again; then reach forward to them, until in the endeavor, he would overbalance himself, and perform an involuntary somerset. Nothing daunted, however, he persevered until he ventured to do what he had been several times on tiptoe to do, leap on the bunch itself; and this he continued to do, though with some failures, holding on in a scrambling way, now by a leaf, now by the berries themselves, until he had rifled the bunch of the ripest. After I had kept him about a week, during which his liveliness and good temper had much attached him to me, though he made not the slightest effort at song, I took him out to cleanse the feathers of his breast from the dried blood that had flowed from his wound. I gently rubbed them with a soft, wet sponge, but whether he took cold, or whether I irritated the wound, I know not; but on being returned to the cage, he instantly began to breathe asthmatically with open beak, apparently with pain, interrupted now and then by fits of coughing, which continued all night, and on the next morning he died. On dissection, I could not find that the shot had penetrated the chest, but they were imbedded in the muscles of the forearm, and had broken the scapula.

"A nest, reported to be of the Cashew Bird, was brought to me on the 18th of June, taken from a pimento-tree. It was a thick, circular mat, slightly concave, of a loose but soft texture, principally composed of cotton, decayed leaves, epidermis of weeds, slender stalks, and tendrils of passion-flower, intermingled, but scarcely interwoven. I think it probable that this had been sustained by a firmer framework; and that the person who took it merely tore out the soft lining as a bed on which the eggs might be carried. The child who brought it could give no account of this. The eggs were two, long-oval, taper at the smaller end; $1\frac{1}{10}$ inch by nearly $\frac{8}{10}$; white, sparingly dashed with irregular, dusky spots in a rude ring around the larger end. The embryo was at this time formed."

The Bahama Finch is known to the inhabitants by the name of Banana Bird, and they seem to apply this name indiscriminately to all the smaller fruit-eating birds with which they happen to be unacquainted. I was informed by a wise old negro that this species was the true Paroquet, and that the "little feller," as he designated the Black-faced Finch, was the Banana Bird. Upon my showing him a female specimen, he appeared slightly puzzled, but after a moment's reflection said it was a Banana Bird, "but of another kind." On one occasion I met a negro who recognized it by the name of Cashew or Casha, a name given it by the inhabitants of Jamaica.

This is the *Fringilla bahamensis* of Catesby.

FAM. ICTERIDÆ.

STARLINGS.

DOLICHONYX ORYZIVORUS. (*Linn.*)

BOBOLINK.

Adult Male. — General plumage, black; patch on the base of the skull, buff; scapulars, rump, and upper tail-coverts, white; primaries edged with yellowish; tail feathers very acute.

Fall Plumage, Male and Female. — Above, yellowish brown, streaked with black or dark brown; under parts, yellowish.

Length 6.50, wing 3.60, tail 2.55, tarsus .95.

I have never met with the Bobolink in the Bahamas, but include it on Dr. Bryant's authority, who says: "On the evening of the 6th of May, towards sunset, I saw a number of flocks of birds flying to the westward, and counted nine in all. This was on Friday. The next day the country was filled with Rice Birds, as they are called there, and boys and men in large numbers turned out to shoot them. I examined a quantity of them, all of which were males in full plumage. Numerous flocks still continued to arrive during this day and Sunday. On Monday, among those shot, were many females. On Tuesday only a few were to be seen, and on Wednesday they had entirely disappeared."

Fig. Aud. Bds. N. A., Vol. IV. pl. 211.

AGELÆUS PHŒNICEUS. Vieil.

Red-winged Blackbird.

Adult Male. — General plumage, black; lesser wing-coverts, bright scarlet, broadly edged with yellowish white; bill and feet, black.

Adult Female. — Above, brownish, the feathers edged with dull rufous or tawny; under parts, dull white, streaked with brown; throat and superciliary line, tawny. (From specimen taken in the United States.)

Female specimens of *A. assimilis*, from Cuba, which I consider to be simply a small southern variety of the present species, are dull black.

Length 8.75, wing 4.40, tail 3.90, tarsus 1.20, bill .80.

The Red-winged Blackbird is a rather common winter visitant, and *perhaps* a resident, as I have taken specimens as late as May 20. We found it quite abundant around the ponds near Hawk's Nest, Andros Island. Nothing peculiar was observed regarding its habits. Its food consists mainly of various kinds of insects and larvæ, of which it destroys great numbers. It also eats fruit and berries.

Fig. Aud. Bds. N. A., Vol. IV. pl. 216.

FAM. TYRANNIDÆ.

FLYCATCHERS.

TYRANNUS MAGNIROSTRIS. d'Orb.
GREAT-BILLED FLYCATCHER.

The present species may be easily identified by its broad bill and large size, being much larger than any other species of this family found in the Bahamas. I have never met with it, and include it simply on the authority of Dr. Bryant, who states that he procured a single specimen at Inagua.

TYRANNUS CAUDIFASCIATUS. (d'Orb.)

I have never met with this species in the Bahamas, but include it provisionally on the authority of Dr. Bryant, who states that he procured a single specimen at Nassau, N. P., during his second visit to the islands.

TYRANNUS GRISEUS. Vieil.
GRAY FLYCATCHER.

Adult Male. — Above, grayish ash, darkest on the head; a dull black patch behind the eye; under parts, whitish; ashy on the sides of the breast; wings, brown; secondaries and coverts edged with dull white; under wing-coverts, pale yellow; tail, brown; feathers faintly tipped and edged with dull white; upper tail-coverts edged with pale rufous.

Length 8.50, wing 4.75, tail 3.75, tarsus .48, bill 1, broad and stout.

This Flycatcher is an abundant summer visitor, and perhaps a resident. After May 15, we found it common on all the islands south of New Providence. Never having found its nest, I am unable to state anything regarding its breeding habits. Its food consists principally of insects of different species, which it pursues and catches with great dexterity.

MIARCHUS STOLIDUS VAR. LEUCAYSIENSIS. (*Gosse.*) *Bryant.*
RUFOUS-TAILED FLYCATCHER.

Winter Plumage, Male.—Above, brownish olive, becoming darker upon the head, and shading into rufous on the rump; under parts, ashy white, shading into yellowish upon the abdomen and crissum; wings, dark brown, the coverts tipped and edged with dull white, forming two wing-bands; the basal half of the outer webs of the primaries, except the first two, edged with rufous, some of the secondaries edged with white; under wing-coverts, pale yellowish white; tail, dark brown, the feathers bordered with rufous upon the inner webs, very faintly upon the two central ones; legs and bill, black. One specimen showed the base of the mandible pale. Female similar to the male.

Length 6.15, wing 2.25, tail 3.35, tarsus .90, bill .70.

The present species is a resident, but is by no means as abundant as some others of its family. Although I have included it as a variety, I am inclined to think that it should be regarded as a distinct species, it being larger, and differing clearly in coloration from *M. stolidus* of Jamaica. Its food consists principally of insects.

CONTOPUS BAHAMENSIS. (*Bryant.*)
LEAST BAHAMA FLYCATCHER.

Winter Plumage, Male. — Above, brownish olive, becoming darker upon the crown; a nearly complete circle of white around the eye, broken above; lores, ashy; below, pale yellow, with a faint tinge of olive; wings, dark brown; under coverts, pale orange-yellow; coverts, secondaries, and tertiaries, brownish white, the coverts forming two indistinct bands upon the wing; tail, dark brown, lighter on the outer feathers; legs and upper mandible, black; lower mandible, pale, becoming darker at tip. One specimen taken had the yellow of the breast much brighter and deeper, the crissum much brighter, the olive markings heavier, and the under wing-coverts *pinkish*. Female resembles the male.

Length 5.35, wing 2.80, tail 2.60, tarsus .58, bill .60.

This little Flycatcher is a resident, and quite abundant in some localities. One morning I observed a bird of this species perched upon a small dead branch. Concealing myself, I watched him, and observed him suddenly dart into the air in pursuit of a small insect, which he captured, and returned at once to his post of observation. This act was repeated again and again, he always returning to the same branch. The stomachs of all the specimens which I examined contained nothing but the remains of small insects. This species is rarely to be found in collections, and is almost unknown to naturalists. The curiously colored specimen mentioned in the description differed from the others which I procured, but not sufficiently, in my opinion, to characterize it as a separate species, as birds of the same species, belonging to this family, often vary in coloration.

PITANGUS BAHAMENSIS. Bryant.

BAHAMA KINGBIRD.

Local Name. — Fighter.

Winter Plumage, Male. — Above, gray, with a tinge of olive on the back; top of the head, including the eye, dark slate-color, concealing a patch of bright orange-yellow upon the crown; under parts ashy white, shading into an olive tinge upon the flanks, and *pale yellow upon the abdomen and crissum;* wings, dark brown, edged with yellowish white, the coverts with pale brown; under wing-coverts, pale yellow; tail, dark brown; outer webs of first two and tips of the rest, brownish white; upper tail-coverts edged with rufous; bill and feet, black. Female similar to male.

Length 8.10, wing 4.20, tail 3.50, tarsus .80, bill .96.

The Fighter, as it is called by the inhabitants, is a constant resident in these islands, and is very abundant. Its habits resemble those of our common Kingbird (*Tyrannus carolinensis*). Dr. Bryant considered this Flycatcher a constant resident, and found it equally abundant in spring and winter. He also says, " Its flight is both powerful and rapid, and it frequently swoops from its perch like a Hawk on some object on the ground. I took from the stomach of one an Anolis six inches in length."

During the summer it was much less common than in winter. Whether it migrates elsewhere, or remains, concealed in the thick underbrush during the warm weather, I was unable to determine.

FAM. CAPRIMULGIDÆ.

GOATSUCKERS.

ANTROSTOMUS CAROLINENSIS. (Gm.)

CHUCK-WILLS-WIDOW.

Local Name.— Death Bird.

Winter Plumage, Male. — Lateral filaments to the bristles of the mouth; general color, pale rufous, mottled with reddish brown; crown streaked with black, feathers of the throat paler and having the appearance of a brownish bar; terminal two thirds of the tail-feathers, with the exception of the four central ones, rufous-white; outer webs mottled to the tips; quills mottled and barred with reddish brown; females showing much more dull white upon the tail.

Length 11.50, wing 8.25, tail 5.50, tarsus .64, bill .50, upper mandible along the edge 1.80.

This rare and interesting species is found during the winter on many of the islands. My first specimen was procured at Long Bay Key, Andros Island, on the 14th of January. It cannot be considered at all common, and it is rarely seen on account of its nocturnal habits. It remains concealed during the daytime, only issuing from its hiding-places when night has set in; then, and not until then, does it go in quest of its food, which consists mainly of insects. It has a peculiar cry, resembling the syllables, "chuck-wills-widow," from which it has received its name. It is probable that some birds remain in the Bahamas throughout the year, as they are merely summer migrants to the United States.

While at Inagua, I was constantly told of a strange and frightful bird, that occasionally was to be seen in the town. The negroes stated that it never appeared until night, and that wherever it was seen, a person in that vicinity would suddenly die, within a short time of its appearance. A vessel was anchored near us at the time, whose crew were dying of yellow fever. The mate had died on shore a few days before, and the captain was then very ill. The negroes cheerfully announced that before the mate's death, and since that time, a Death Bird had been seen every night in that vicinity. My curiosity being aroused, I procured a negro guide, and arming myself with a light shot-gun, started for the spot where the Death Bird had last been seen. It was a beautiful night with a full moon, and I had great hopes of procuring a specimen, if we were lucky enough to see one. On the way my guide entertained me with accounts of the doings of this interesting species. He stated that a few months before, the bird had appeared to an old man, whose death occurred a few days afterwards; also, that if we saw it, a death would take place shortly after. I hastened to assure him that the last statement was undoubtedly true, and that if we saw a Death Bird something would die shortly after, but in all probability it would be the bird. From some reason, perhaps because the bird was not bloodthirsty that night, he did not appear, and so I was unable to determine its species. From the descriptions of the bird that were given me, I believed it to be the present species, and my belief was strengthened by the fact that the inhabitants of Andros Island seemed to know it by that name; but the natives of Inagua say that it perches itself on a tree soon after dark, and repeatedly utters a cry commencing loudly, then softly to itself before again uttering its loud note, thus: Coo-cu-cu-cu-cu-Coo. This note does not at all resemble the cry of *A. Carolinensis*, while it does resemble very much that of the *Nyctibius jamaicensis*, as described by Gosse; and it is possible that the Inagua bird may be that species.

CHORDEILES MINOR. Cab.
Little Nighthawk.

Local Name. — Pira-mi-dink.

Adult Male. — Above, dark brown, variegated with white and tawny; under parts, tawny, banded with brown; throat, tawny, becoming whitish on the breast; a white line from sides of the throat to chin; first two primaries with a spot on the inner web, and the second and third with a band of white; edge of corpus white.

Length 7, wing 6.40, tail 3.70, bill .28, tarsus .44.

The Pira-mi-dink appears to be as abundant in the Bahama Islands as our common species is with us. In their habits they closely resemble each other, but their notes are very different. About sunset they are to be seen flying swiftly about, in search of insects, occasionally uttering the peculiar cry from which they have derived their local name. At Inagua it was quite common, and I was fortunate enough to find it breeding. A single egg was deposited upon the sand without any attempt at a nest. Occasionally, I have observed them in large flocks flying low over the land, and when together they are generally silent. None remain during the winter. This is the species which Dr. Bryant thought to be *Chordeiles popetue*, as he says: "They began to arrive about the 1st of May, and were numerous by the 10th."

The egg bears a close resemblance to that of our common species (*C. popetue*), but has somewhat more of a purplish tinge, and is smaller and paler.

FAM. TROCHILIDÆ.

HUMMING-BIRDS.

DORICHA EVELYNÆ. (*Bourc.*)

BAHAMA WOODSTAR.

Local Name. — Hummer.

Winter Plumage, Male. — Above, green, showing slight golden reflections on the back, with the tips of the feathers in some specimens bluish; head darker; throat, beautiful purple-violet, below which is a band of white; under parts, green, mixed with rufous, shading into white on the flanks; crissum, pale rufous-white; wings, brownish purple; tail appearing black, very dark purple in some lights; outer feathers with faint terminal spot of rufous, second with inner web, and third with inner and basal half of outer web cinnamon; bill and feet, black.

Winter Plumage, Female. — Purple gorget wanting, and replaced by dull white, with a slight tinge of rufous; upper parts paler than in the male; sides, cinnamon, becoming brightest under the wings; central feathers of the tail, bright green, the rest cinnamon; an oblique purplish band on the tips of the fourth feathers.

Length 3.40, wing 1.70, tail 1.40, tarsus .15, bill .70.

The Bahama Islands are the home of this beautiful little Humming-bird. It is very abundant in the neighborhood of Nassau, where I procured a fine series of specimens. Dr. Bryant gives an interesting account of this species. He says, "All the specimens I procured, seven in number, were killed in February and the early part of March. At that time its food consisted almost entirely of a small green apkis, found abundantly in the West India vervain (*V. stachytarpheta*), a small blue flower that grows in all the dry pastures. Gosse calls the Least Humming-bird of Jamaica the Vervain Humming-bird from its hovering round the plant, but the name would apply as well to the present species. I saw nothing in its habits differing from those of the common ruby-throated species, with the exception that it was more quarrelsome in its disposition, chasing the Fighter, as the *Tyrannus caudifasciatus* is called, whenever it came near him, and that its note is louder and shriller than that of our species, and much more frequently uttered.

"Incubation commences by the 1st of March. I saw three nests of this bird. One found on the 3d of March contained two eggs, partly hatched; a second, April 10, one egg; and another in May, two eggs. The nests were all composed of the same materials, principally the cotton from the silk-cotton tree, with a few downy masses that looked as if derived from some species of asclepias. This was felted and matted together, and the outside stuck over with bits of lichens and little dry stalks or fibres of vegetable matter.... The eggs, like those of all others of the family, are but two in number, snow-white when blown, and slightly rosy before."

If Dr. Bryant's account of this species is correct, it does not appear to have any regular breeding season, as I have taken its nest and eggs in June, and was shown two nests which were taken by a gentleman near Nassau in the month of December.

Their flight is very rapid, as they dart from place to place in a sudden, jerky sort of way; while hovering over a flower, the movement of the wings is so rapid that it is impossible to follow them with the eye, producing a slight humming sound, from which the bird has derived its name.

Fig Gould's Mon. Trochil., Vol. III.

DORICHA LYRURA. Gould.
LYRE-TAILED HUMMING-BIRD.

Adult Male.— General appearance the same as *D. evelynæ*, but differs from it by showing the beautiful *purple violet on the forehead* as well as on the throat, and also having a much longer tail, formed somewhat in the shape of a lyre, from which this bird has derived its name. The throat of *D. lyrura* shows *bright blue*, in some lights, on the lower part, while that of *D. evelynæ* is almost entirely purple-violet, showing the bluish tinge very slightly if at all.

Length 3.64, wing 1.60, tail 1.58, tarsus .13, bill .60.

Like many others of its family, the Lyre-tailed Humming-bird is restricted to a single island. It inhabits Inagua, and although not rare, cannot be considered as an abundant species. All the specimens which I procured were killed near Mathewstown, and none were taken on any other part of the island. Its habits, as far as I was able to observe, were the same as those of *D. evelynæ*, from which it is impossible to distinguish it while darting from one flower to another. A negro brought me a fine male alive, which he had caught in a small net as it hovered over a flower. When living, the plumage shows somewhat brighter than in a dead specimen.

SPORADINUS RICORDI. (d'Orb.)
Ricord's Humming-bird.

Winter Plumage, Male. — Entire plumage, bronzy green, becoming metallic on the throat; wings, purplish brown; four central tail-feathers bronze, the remainder purplish black, showing bronze on the outer webs; under tail-coverts, white; upper mandible, dark brown; lower mandible pale, becoming dark at the tip; tail forked.

Winter Plumage, Female. — Resembles the male, except having the crown brownish; throat and centre of abdomen, pale buff; under tail-coverts, grayish white.

Length 3.60, wing 1.80, tail 1.50, tarsus .15, bill .75.

I was agreeably surprised at finding this pretty little species common on Andros Island, as it had not been previously recorded from the Bahamas. It seemed to prefer the vicinity of the shore, as none were taken far inland, and was quite abundant in the neighborhood of Long Bay Key, as was also *D. evelynæ*.

On the 13th of January, my friend, Mr. George E. Fowle, Jr., found the nest of this species near Long Bay Key. It was attached to a small trailing vine, which was suspended from the branch of a paw-paw tree, about four feet from the ground. The nest was close to the branch, and contained two young birds, apparently about a week old.

The young were dark slate-color above, with the under parts flesh-color, having a slight down upon the back; the bill was fully as broad as it was long, having the upper mandible dark, and the lower light colored.

Mr. Gould, in his magnificent monograph of this family, restricted the range of *S. ricordi* to the island of Cuba, and all other writers have done the same. In Ramon de la Sagra's " Histoire de Cuba" is to be found the following note regarding this species: " Far from migrating, like the Red Humming-bird (*Trochilus colubris*), this is one of the stationary inhabitants of the island of Cuba, which it never leaves, and of which it is one of the most beautiful ornaments. The inhabitants (to imitate, doubtless, the sound which it makes while flying) give it the name of *Zun-zun*. Interesting in its plumage and habits, its works likewise are not without merit. Artificially built, and often composed of wool from the silk which surrounds the seed of *Asclepias anasarica*, its nest is attached to the forks of young twigs; like that of all the *Trochilidæ*, it contains only one or two eggs, from which the young are produced, which, at their birth, have the beak very short."

This Humming-bird approaches very closely the next species, so closely, in fact, that were it not for the high authority which has separated them I should not be inclined to consider them distinct.

Fig. Gould's Mon. Trochil., Vol. V.

SPORADINUS BRACEI. Lawr.
BRACE'S HUMMING-BIRD.

Male. — Crown and gorget of a glittering pale green; back, upper tail-coverts, the two central and the next pair of tail-feathers, bronzed golden green; the other tail-feathers are purplish black, with their outer edges bronzed green; quills, blackish purple; breast and abdomen, dull bronzy green; under tail-coverts, dark ash, bordered with white; bill and feet, black.

Length 3.37, wing 1.75, tail 1.12, bill .75.

I include this as a species on the authority of Mr. George N. Lawrence, and have given his description of it in detail. In his report regarding it he says, " The specimen is a mummy, and the outer two tail-feathers are just being renewed; the length of these is important to determine its true generic position; but as it resembles *Sporadinus ricordii* in other respects, I place it provisionally in the same genus. If the outer tail-feathers were fully developed, they would doubtless increase the total length as well as that of the tail. This species is nearly allied to *S. ricordii* from Cuba, but differs from it in being smaller, with a longer bill; the green of the crown and throat is paler and a more steely shade; the back is more bronzed, and the under plumage of a lighter green."

The type was taken near Nassau, N. P., by Mr. L. J. K. Brace, and is the only specimen known to be in existence.

FAM. ALCEDINIDÆ.

KINGFISHERS.

CERYLE ALCYON. (Linn.)
BELTED KINGFISHER.

Adult Male. — Above, ashy blue; head with crest, throat, band around the neck, a spot anterior to the eye, belly and crissum. white; a band across the breast and sides of the body the color of the back; primaries with white on the basal half; tail with bands and spots of white.

Adult Female. — Easily distinguished from the male by having the sides of the body and a band across the upper part of the belly. light chestnut.

Length 12.50, wing 6, tail 3.65, tarsus .36, bill 2.

The Kingfisher becomes common during the winter, generally frequenting the small lakes and ponds in the interior of the islands. I rarely visited Lake Cunningham, in the neighborhood of Nassau, without observing one or more of this species. Dr. Bryant found it common during the winter, but did not observe any after April 1.

Fig. Aud. Bds. N. A., Vol. IV. pl. 255.

FAM. CUCULIDÆ.

CUCKOOS.

SAUROTHERA BAHAMENSIS. Bryant.

BAHAMA CUCKOO.

Adult. — Above, pale olive, showing slight greenish reflections; throat and breast dull grayish white; belly and crissum, tawny; primaries, mostly rufous; tail-feathers, except the two central ones, tipped with pale brownish white; legs, slaty blue; soles of the feet, yellow; eyelids, vermilion red; upper mandible, brownish, shading into slate-color at the base; iris, brown.

Length 18, wing 6.25, tail 9.50, tarsus 1.50, bill 1.80.

I met with this bird but once. A single specimen taken at Nassau, June 17. Dr. Bryant states that it was quite abundant during his visits, and that the inhabitants called it Rain Crow. In this I think that he was mistaken in the species, as the negroes who saw my specimen considered it to be the same as *C. minor*, "only full grown." It is a curious fact that Dr. Bryant did not meet with *C. minor*, while I found it abundant on many of the islands. He also says, "Its food during the winter consisted principally of a species

of Phasma, found in great abundance in the leaves of the air plants. This bird is one of the tamest, considering its size, that I am acquainted with. I have frequently watched them searching for insects within two or three feet of my head." Nothing is known regarding its breeding habits.

COCCYZUS AMERICANUS. (*Linn.*)
YELLOW-BILLED CUCKOO.

Adult Male. — Above, metallic olive-green; *under parts*, white; outer tail-feathers tipped with white; *upper mandible* and tip of lower, black, the rest of the lower mandible, yellow; iris, brown. Female similar to the male.

Length 12, wing 5.90, tail 6.30.

Mr. L. J. K. Brace informed me that he had taken this Cuckoo in the vicinity of Nassau. It probably visits the islands occasionally during the winter.

Fig. Aud. Bds. N. A., Vol. IV. pl. 275.

COCCYZUS MINOR. (*Gm.*)
MANGROVE CUCKOO.

Winter Plumage, Male. — Above, grayish olive, tinged with ash on the head; under parts, yellowish brown, darkest on the thighs, and becoming pale on the throat; a streak of dark brown behind the eye, passing under it; quills and under wing-coverts, yellowish brown; outer tail-feathers, black, tipped with white, and showing slight bronze reflections, the others lighter, except the central ones, tipped with white; under mandible, yellow, except at the tip. Female similar to the male.

Length 12, wing 5.45, tail 6.50, tarsus 1.04, bill 1.

The Mangrove Cuckoo, so rare in the United States, is rather abundant on the larger islands of the Bahamas. It was common in the neighborhood of Nassau, although generally keeping well concealed in the thick undergrowth. It remains throughout the year, and during the breeding season constructs a rough nest resembling that of our common species, in which it lays three and sometimes four eggs, of a greenish color. The nest is generally placed in a low bush near the ground, and is very loosely constructed.

Fig. Aud. Bds. N. A., Vol. IV. pl. 272.

CROTOPHAGA ANI. (*Linn.*)
ANI.

Local Names. — Rain Crow, Blackbird.

Winter Plumage, Male. — Upper mandible much curved; culmen rising above the head, flattened to a sharp edge; nostrils situated in the middle of the lower half of the upper mandible. General color black, showing bluish reflections; the feathers of the head, neck, breast, and upper part of the back with metallic bronze borders; iris, brown. Female, similar.

Length 13.25, wing 6, tail 8, tarsus 1.25, bill 1.20.

The Ani, or Blackbird, as it is sometimes called by the inhabitants, is a very abundant resident in the Bahamas. Its habits much resemble those of our common Grackle. They are generally observed in flocks, feeding in the fields or perched upon the branches of a bush, uttering from time to time a curious, but not unmusical whistle. They appear to eat almost anything that comes in their way, insects of various kinds, beetles, berries, or fruits being equally acceptable.

Incubation commences about the 1st of December, and we procured specimens of fully fledged young birds in January. It is probable that they rear two broods in a season, as Mr. Gosse found a nest containing eggs in July. He says, " In July I found a Blackbird's nest in a bastard cedar; it was a rather large mass of interwoven twigs, lined with leaves. Eight eggs were in the nest, and the shells of many more were also in it and scattered beneath the tree. The eggs were about as large as a pullet's, very regularly oval, of a greenish blue, but covered with a coating of white chalky substance, which was much scratched and eroded on them all, and which was displaced with a little force."

Although very abundant around Nassau, they become quite scarce on many of the more southern islands, and it is considered a rare bird at Inagua.

Bd. Bwr. and Ridg., Vol. II.

FAM. PICIDÆ.

WOODPECKERS.

PICUS VILLOSUS, Linn.

HAIRY WOODPECKER.

Winter Plumage, Male. — Above, black, with a white band down the middle of the back finely lined with black; all the quills, middle and larger wing-coverts, with numerous spots of white; crown, a black patch over the eye, and a stripe from the mandible to the nape, white; a black stripe from the eye, passing through the cheeks, over the nape, and joining the black of the back; a scarlet crescent around the base of the skull, joining the white superciliary stripe; under parts, ashy, with the sides mottled and striped with black; two outer tail feathers white, edged and tipped with pale brown; third, black, with a patch of pale brown upon the outer web, the others black. Female, the scarlet crescent wanting, replaced by white.

Length 7.25, wing 4.20, tail 3, tarsus .70, bill 1.

The Hairy Woodpecker is occasionally found in the Bahamas during the winter season. At Nassau it was rather common, but by no means as abundant as *S. varius*. Its food consists of insects, berries, and small fruits.

Fig. Aud. Bds. N. A., Vol. IV. pl. 262.

SPHYRAPICUS VARIUS. (Linn.)
YELLOW-BELLIED WOODPECKER.

Winter Plumage, Male. — Above, black, variegated with brown and dull white, becoming dull white on the upper tail-coverts; crown, crimson (often interrupted with brownish), bordered by a narrow line of black; a streak above the eye and a broader one from the bill, passing below the eye and down the neck to sides of the breast, yellowish white; ends of wing-coverts, white, forming a broad bar; quills spotted with white; throat, crimson, with a band of intermixed black and brown upon the breast; sides, light brown mottled with black; belly, pale yellow; inner tail-feathers edged with dull white; outer feathers edged with white, becoming light brown at the tips.

Winter Plumage, Female. — Above, black, variegated with white and light brown; crown, crimson, mottled with light brown, and bordered narrowly with black at the nape; a dull brownish white stripe passing from the base of the bill under the eye to the sides of the neck; *throat, dull brownish white,* becoming brown on the breast; sides mottled with black; belly, pale yellow. Immature birds, without black on the breast or red on the head, and in every intermediate stage to the adult.

Length 8.35, wing 4.75, tail 3.20, tarsus .70, bill .96.

The Yellow-bellied Woodpecker becomes abundant in the neighborhood of Nassau during the winter season. We often observed them clinging to the trunks of the trees, or flying over the road during our excursions to and from different parts of the island. It did not appear to show any decided preference for any particular kind of tree, as has been stated by some writers; but seemed to wander aimlessly about in search of its food, which consists of insects and berries, although it often eats the sap of the trees, which it procures by drilling holes through the bark with its strong, sharp bill, in many cases killing the tree.

Fig. Aud. Bds. N. A., Vol. IV. pl. 267.

FAM. PSITTACIDÆ.

PARROTS.

CHRYSOTIS COLLARIA. (*Linn.*)

PARROT.

Adult Male.— General plumage, green, many feathers narrowly tipped with dark brown; forehead, and the top of the head to the eyes, white; throat, bright red, sometimes touched with green; some of the feathers on the belly, brownish red; outer webs of primaries, blue, inner webs, brown; tail, green, showing blue on outer webs of outer feathers, and red on the basal half of inner webs of all except the central ones, which sometimes show a trace near the shaft; bill, yellowish white; iris, brown.

Length 13, wing 8, tail 4.50, tarsus .75, bill 1.25.

Many years ago the Parrot was abundant throughout the Bahamas, but at the present time it is common only at Inagua. The natives claim that they also exist at Abaco and Long Island, but if this be true, it is probably only in small numbers, as we never met with them during our explorations of the last-named islands. I was told that during the month of July they repair in large numbers to the cornfields near Mathewstown and cause great destruction to the crops. At this season they become quite tame, and quantities of them are killed by the negroes. We found them abundant near Northwest Point during the month of June, but at that time they were very shy and difficult to shoot. The natives capture them when young, and they become very tame and learn to speak quickly.

One afternoon, while shooting in the vicinity of Northwest Point, Inagua, I suddenly came upon a large flock of Parrots, which flew from one tree to another, uttering harsh cries as I approached One specimen which I shot was merely wing-tipped, and with the aid of my coat I was enabled to capture the little fellow, without giving him a chance to use his bill, which, from the way he screamed and struggled, he evidently had a great desire to do. He lived for several days, and became quite docile; but one morning being left alone, his curiosity prompted him to explore among some freshly poisoned skins, and upon my return I found him lying dead upon the floor of the cabin.

The eggs of this species are generally deposited in a hollow tree. The negroes say that of late years the nest is rarely found, as the birds repair to the interior of the island to breed.

FAM. STRIGIDÆ.

OWLS.

STRIX FLAMMEA VAR. PRATINCOLA. (*Linn.*) *Bp.*

BARN OWL.

Adult Male. — Above, tawny brown, delicately mottled in places with black and white; under parts showing pale tawny, dotted with brown; face, whitish, with an ante-orbital of brown; under surface of wings, white, slightly dotted with brown; tail, with four black bars on the upper surface below, pale.

Length 15.25, wing 13, tail 5.70, tarsus 2.75.

The Barn Owl is a resident in the Bahamas, and is claimed to be abundant by the inhabitants, who know it by a variety of names, among which are Monkey-faced Owl, Brown Owl, White Owl, and a dozen others about as applicable. I was able to procure only two specimens during my stay, one of which was kindly presented to me by Mr. Epes Sargent, of Nassau. Mr. N. B. Moore found a pair of this species breeding in the vicinity of Nassau, N. P. He says, "The nest is in a niche in a perpendicular (vertical) wall of rock, thirty feet from the base and fifteen feet below the top, and is unapproachable. I killed one of a pair of this species, a female, as she entered the niche. The male, her mate, on the following night entered it, uttering his peculiar call-note; an owl soon approached, he gave chase, they flew about for some time, and on the next night they were, to all appearance, mated. Had the male been killed instead of the female, this sudden marriage, and particularly *her* continuance at the old nesting-place, would seem less surprising. This species has two very distinct vocal utterances,—one a 'call-note,' a sort of low, rapid chattering or clacking, uttered, so far as I have observed, when perched; the other a monosyllabic note, which I would spell 'creech,' uttered in a harsh half-scream, while on the wing, the intervals being very long."

Its food consists of mice and other small quadrupeds, and according to some writers, small birds.

The inhabitants of some of the islands claim that a large, *pure white* owl is sometimes seen; but in all probability it is the present species, which they have seen flying about in the dim light of the evening.

Fig. Aud. Bds. N. A., Vol. I. pl. 34.

SPHEOTYTO CUNICULARIA VAR. FLORIDANA. (Mol.) Ridg.

FLORIDA BURROWING OWL.

Adult Male. — General plumage, *dark brown*, mottled with white; under parts, paler; feathers barred with brown and white, shading into pale tawny near the vent; primaries, reddish brown, blotched with dull white and pale tawny; tail-feathers, brown, barred with white, the bars not reaching the shafts; *tarsus feathered in front and very long;* bill, brown, light at tip; claws, black.

Length 10, wing 6.50, tail 3, tarsus 1.60, bill .75.

Mr. L. J. K. Brace procured this species at Nassau, N. P., and it is probably found on some of the other islands. The inhabitants seemed to be acquainted with a small owl, but their statements concerning it were very unsatisfactory. Mr. Brace states regarding this species: "For about a month past, I had been watching a small owl that was in the habit of foraging up and down the wharves that line one side of the harbor of Nassau. As dusk approached he would make his appearance, and perch on some elevated place, such as a post or part of a fence. On the approach of any one to his resting-place, he would allow them to come within twenty feet, but if approached nearer, no matter how cautiously, he would fly off, generally uttering a shrill, quickly reiterated chur-chur-chur-chut! to another spot, scarcely ever returning to the same one. Some evenings he was more vociferous than on others. I could not determine when he returned during the day; but he would generally arrive from a southerly inland direction, at other times from either the east or west end of the wharves. When shot, he had only come a short time, and was perched on the cross-trees of a flag-staff, about fifteen feet high. From part of the contents of the gizzard, I concluded it was attracted by the 'Crawlers,' a species of Ligia that abounds on the sides of the wharves; it also contained the half-digested remains of a Hyla."

FAM. FALCONIDÆ.

FALCONS.

CIRCUS CYANEUS VAR. HUDSONIUS. (*Linn.*)
Marsh Hawk.

Adult Male.— Above, ashy; primaries, brownish at the end; upper tail-coverts, white.

Female. — Above, brown, streaked with reddish; tail barred. This species is easily distinguished by the white upper tail-coverts.

Length 16, wing 13, tail 9.10, tarsus 2.80, bill .60.

According to Dr. Bryant, this species occasionally visits the Bahamas. He procured a single specimen, in immature plumage, at Inagua. None were observed by our party.

Fig. Aud. Bds. N. A., Vol. I. pl. 26.

ACCIPITER FUSCUS. (*Gm.*)
Sharp-shinned Hawk.

Adult Male.— Above, plumbeous; tail, brownish, banded with brownish black and tipped with whitish; under parts, white, streaked and banded with pale rufous, darkest on the breast.

Length 10, wing 6.50, tail 5.60, tarsus 1.75.

The Sharp-shinned Hawk is not uncommon during the winter. It was occasionally seen near Nassau, which was the only place where we observed it. Dr. Bryant considered it the most common species.

Fig. Aud. Bds. N. A., Vol. I. pl. 25.

FALCO COMMUNIS. (Gm.)
PEREGRINE FALCON.

Adult Male. — Above, blackish, feathers becoming gray on the back, and gray mottled with dark slate on the rump; a black cheek-patch; throat and breast, dull white; lower part of the breast narrowly streaked with brown; belly, flanks, sides of the body, and under wing-coverts, whitish, showing a tinge of tawny, banded and streaked with brown; tail, alternately banded with dark and light slate-color, the feathers tipped with yellowish white; tarsus and feet, yellowish green; claws, black. Female, larger.

Length 17.25, wing 12.50, tail 6.50, tarsus 1.80, bill .80.

This Falcon is by no means common. A single specimen was killed at Norman's Key on January 7. Dr. Bryant found a dead bird of this species at Norman's Key, which proved to be an adult male, in fine spring plumage.

Many naturalists of the present day consider the American Falcon to be a variety of the European bird. In this I think they are wrong, as the differences which have been pointed out as distinguishing characters are very slight, and vary in specimens from different localities. It is claimed that the main point of difference between them is the striped breast of the European bird, which is *generally* wanting in the American specimens; but American specimens are sometimes striped, and I cannot but agree with Mr. Dresser in considering the American and European bird as inseparable.

Fig. Aud. Bds. N. A., Vol. I. pl. 20.

FALCO SPARVERIUS. (*Linn.*)
Sparrow Falcon.

Adult Male. — Crown, ashy blue, sometimes replaced by chestnut in the centre; a maxillary and auricular black stripe; back, brown, sometimes spotted with black on the lower part; wing-coverts, bluish ash; tail, reddish brown, with a band of black tipped with white, sometimes showing several black bands; below, white, showing reddish brown on the breast and belly.

Adult Female. — Upper parts, lighter than in the male, barred with dull black; under parts, dull yellowish white, paler than in the male; streaked; otherwise similar.

Length 10, wing 7, tail 4.75.

The present species is included on the authority of Dr. Bryant, who states that he saw two specimens at Nassau and one at Great Stirrup Key. None were observed by our party.

Fig. Aud. Bds. N. A., Vol. I. pl. 22.

BUTEO BOREALIS. (Gm.)
RED-TAILED HAWK.

Adult Male. — Above, dark brown, edged with tawny; tail-coverts, whitish; below, white; the throat streaked with light, and the belly with darker brown, sometimes the belly being but very faintly marked; tail, above, bright chestnut-red, showing a subterminal black band and a terminal white one.

Length 22, wing 15.50, tail 8.50, tarsus 2.10.

I have never met with this species in the Bahamas, but have included it on the authority of Dr. Bryant, who states that two specimens were taken, one at Nassau, and the other at Inagua.

Fig. Aud. Bds. N. A., Vol. I. pl. 7.

PANDION HALIÆTUS. (Linn.)
FISH HAWK.

Winter Plumage, Male. — Above, dark brown; head, white, somewhat marked with dark brown on crown and cheeks, varying in specimens; under parts, white, sometimes streaked with light brown, especially on the breast; feet very large, bluish.

Length 22, wing 18.50, tail 9, tarsus 2.40, bill 1.40.

This species is an abundant resident; we met with it on all of the larger islands. While at Clarence Harbor, Long Island, a fine adult Hawk came regularly every evening and perched himself upon the top of the mainmast, where he would sit quietly, slightly moving his partly closed wings to balance himself as the vessel rolled. Dr. Bryant, writing of this species, says, "Fish Hawks were found throughout the Bahamas, but nowhere so abundant as in parts of the United States. The nests which I saw were placed in entirely different situations from those chosen by this bird with us, resembling more nearly in this respect the European species. They were all built on the ground. Two that I examined at Water Key, Ragged Islands, were placed on the edge of a cliff at an elevation of about forty feet from the water, very bulky, at least five feet in height and six in diameter, composed entirely of materials taken from the neighboring beaches, principally the horny skeletons of gorgonias, sponges, bits of drift-wood, and sea-weeds. They had recently been repaired, and the cavities lined with fresh gulf-weed. On the 20th of April, the date of my last visit to them, they contained neither eggs nor young. The eggs in the ovary of a female shot at this time were of the size of small peas.

"The plumage of the specimen differed from any I ever saw in the United States. The whole upper part of the head, nape, and hind neck was white, without any mixture of brown; no difference was observed in the comparative measurements. I intended to have preserved it, but, unfortunately, before I was ready to skin it, the cook plucked it for his private table."

The food of this species appears to consist almost entirely of fish, which it shows great expertness in catching, — according to some writers plunging entirely beneath the surface in pursuit of its prey. But although I have seen hundreds of birds of this species, and watched them at different times in the act of catching fish, I have never, in a single instance, seen them go entirely under water. The eggs are usually from two to three in number, although some writers claim that they sometimes lay four.

Fig. Aud. Bds. N. A., Vol. I. pl. 15.

FAM. CATHARTIDÆ.

VULTURES.

CATHARTES AURA. (*Linn.*)
TURKEY BUZZARD.

Local Name. — Crow.

Winter Plumage, Male. — Above, marked with brown and black; shafts of the primaries, yellowish externally; under parts, black, becoming brown on the belly; head, red, base showing only a few short, bristly feathers; feet, pinkish; bill, bluish white.

Length 27, wing 21, tail 10, tarsus 2.35.

The Turkey Buzzard is abundant at Andros Island and at Abaco. It is a resident and undoubtedly breeds in the Bahamas. While walking along the beach, near Grassy Creek, Andros Island, I observed a number of these birds perched upon a small tree, and on turning a corner of the rock, suddenly came upon thirteen more of them, feeding upon the body of a dead dog. They did not appear to mind my presence in the least, and it was not until I had approached within a few feet of them that they showed any inclination to leave their prey. Dr. Bryant gives this bird as abundant at

Andros, Abaco, and Grand Bahama, but did not meet with it elsewhere. He writes: "I was for a long while unable to explain satisfactorily to myself the cause of their absence from Nassau, as in the United States they are generally very abundant in the neighborhood of the large Southern cities, as Charleston and Savannah, for instance. This fact, I now think, is owing to their inability to procure food at New Providence. All the animals slaughtered there are literally devoured by the blacks; not a morsel, even to the entrails, is thrown away as offal, so that the slaughter-houses, which at Savannah are their principal feeding-places, do not at Nassau offer them a mouthful of food. The number of domestic animals also running at large on the island is so small, that the carcasses of those dying by disease or accident would only afford them an occasional supply; and the native fauna is so meagre that it is unnecessary to take it into consideration. I passed several days at Grassy Creek, near the southern extremity of Andros Island. This is one of the places where the Black-mouthed Helmet (*Cassis Madagascariensis*), of which cameos are made, is procured. The shells, after being brought on shore, are placed on scaffolds with the mouth downwards, in order that after the death of the animal it may fall out of its own weight. These scaffolds are constantly attended by the Buzzards, and they can frequently be seen tugging at the protruding animal, much to the displeasure of the fishermen, as the birds frequently knock down the shells, and sometimes drag them into the bushes out of sight. The name given to this bird by the inhabitants is 'John Crow,' the same as in Jamaica, according to Gosse. I examined several specimens, but could detect no difference between them and birds obtained in the United States. This is not to be wondered at, as the Gulf Stream is so narrow, that I think when soaring at the greatest height to which they attain, they must be able to see the main-land, and if so, doubtless pass to and fro. No specimen of the *C. jota* was seen."

The Turkey Buzzard generally deposits its eggs in some cleft in the rocks, or on a decayed stump, usually without any attempt at a nest. The eggs are generally two in number.

Fig. Aud. Bds. N. A., Vol. I. pl. 2.

FAM. COLUMBIDÆ.

PIGEONS.

COLUMBA LEUCOCEPHALA. (Linn.)
WHITE-HEADED PIGEON.

Local Name.— Pigeon.

Winter Plumage. Male.— Above, grayish blue, showing slight reflections; crown, pale buff at some seasons pure white, bordered at the nape by a band of dark purple, and below it a cape extending upon each side of the neck, of metallic green, the feathers bordered with black; quills, dark brown, becoming lighter upon the secondaries; under parts, grayish blue; crissum, plumbeous; tail, dark brown. Sexes similar.

Length 13.25, wing 6.90, tail 5.50, tarsus .90, bill .70.

During the winter season the present species is rarely seen, on account of its frequenting the thickly wooded parts of the islands. Occasionally, I saw them in the market at Nassau, but they are by no means common. As soon as the summer season sets in they become gregarious, and repair in immense flocks to the outer keys to breed. Their food consists of berries and small fruits. Incubation commences about May 1.

Dr. Bryant, who found it breeding, says, "It breeds in communities in some places, as at Grassy Key, Andros Island, in vast numbers. Here the nests were made on the tops of the prickly pear, which covers the whole key; at the Biminis and Buena Vista Key, Ragged Islands, on the mangrove, and at Long Rock, near Exuma, on stunted bushes. I do not think they ever select a large key for their breeding-place. The eggs are laid by the middle of May, and the young leave their nests about the 1st of July, previous to which great numbers are killed by the negroes. It is a shy bird, when not breeding, even in the most uninhabited localities."

Fig. Aud. Bds. N. A., Vol. IV. pl. 280.

ZENAIDA AMABILIS. (Bp.)
ZENAIDA DOVE.

Local Name. — Wood Dove.

Adult Male. — Above, olive-brown; top of the head and under parts, pale purplish brown; sides of the body and under wing-coverts, blue; tail-feathers, with the exception of the central ones, bluish, with a black band about an inch from the tip; slight streak of metallic blue below the ear; quills, dark brown; secondaries tipped with white; feet, reddish.

Length 10.50, wing 6, tail 4, tarsus 1, bill .55.

This beautiful Dove is found throughout the Bahamas, but does not appear to be very abundant. It seems to be rather solitary in its habits, and is never met with in flocks. The nest is composed of small sticks, loosely put together. On May 27 I procured a nest which was placed in the crotch of a fallen tree about three feet from the ground. It contained two white eggs.

Dr. Bryant says, "It never collects in flocks, not breeding in communities like the *C. leucocephala.* In its habits it is intermediate between the *Z. carolinensis* and the *C. passerina.* It feeds and passes the principal part of its time on the ground, and when flushed, flies off in a straight line, very much as the common quail. The crops of those killed by me were filled with small seed about the size of mustard-seed, apparently all of the same kind. All the nests I saw were made in holes in the rocks, and consisted, as is always the case in this family, of but a few sticks. It probably migrates farther south during the winter, as it was much more abundant in May than at any previous time."

Fig. Aud. Bds. N. A., Vol. V. pl. 281.

CHAMÆPELIA PASSERINA. (*Linn*)
GROUND DOVE.

Local Name. — Tobacco Dove.

Winter Plumage, Male. — Above, grayish olive, showing a bluish tinge upon the nape and crown; under parts, reddish purple, becoming ashy on the sides; under wing-coverts and quills showing *reddish brown*, the latter margined and tipped with dark brown; middle tail-feathers like the back, the others dark brown; two outer feathers tipped with white; upper surface of wing showing large spots of bluish-purple; bill and feet yellowish, the former becoming dark at the tip.

Length 6.30, wing 3.30, tail 2.60, tarsus .50, bill .50.

This graceful little Dove is a resident, and very abundant everywhere. While walking through a pineapple plantation, I have been astonished at the quantity of these birds which were constantly flying about. They are very tame, and often allowed me to approach within a few feet of them without showing any signs of alarm. Their food consists of seeds and many kinds of small berries. I have often watched them dusting themselves in the warm sand of the road, after the manner of our farm-yard fowls, seeming to enjoy it greatly. Incubation commences about May 15. A nest taken at the Miraporvos, May 27, contained two eggs, which were quite fresh. It was simply a little mat of grass, loosely put together, placed upon the ground in an open space, concealed only by short marsh-grass, barely high enough to hide the bird when sitting upon the nest. The eggs are white.

Fig. Aud. Bds. N. A., Vol. V. pl. 283.

GEOTRYGON MARTINICA. (Gm.)
Key West Dove.

Winter Plumage, Male. — Above, chestnut-rufous; crown and neck with metallic reflections of green and purple; back showing brilliant purple, reflections becoming less distinct on the rump; a band of white from the base of the lower mandible under the eye to the side of the neck, bordered below by a streak of dull purple; under parts showing the breast pale purple, becoming dull white on the throat and abdomen; primaries, bright rufous, becoming darker at the tips; tail, rufous; legs, red.

Length 10.75, wing 6, tail 4.30, tarsus 1, bill .90.

This beautiful Pigeon is an abundant resident. It is to be met with in small flocks, and generally inhabits the heavily wooded parts of the islands. They remain concealed during the heat of the day, but early in the morning often come out into the open ground to feed. On several occasions I saw birds of this species exhibited for sale at the market in Nassau, and had the good fortune to procure several very fine specimens which were brought in by the negroes. The note is low and mournful, and is often heard during the early hours of the morning.

Fig. Aud. Bds. N. A., Vol. V. pl. 282.

FAM. PERDICIDÆ.

PARTRIDGES.

ORTYX VIRGINIANUS. (Linn.)
PARTRIDGE.

Local Name. — Quail.

Winter Plumage, Male. — Above, rich brownish red, mottled with black; crown, black, shading into brown at the base of the skull, and mottled with black and white on the nape; a white superciliary line passing from nostril to nape; throat, white, bordered broadly with black; upper breast and sides, reddish brown, shading into white on the belly, the feathers thickly banded with black; crissum, reddish brown; tertials and some of the wing-coverts edged with yellowish white; bill, entirely black.

Winter Plumage, Female. — Resembles the male; the white of the head and throat replaced by tawny, without black edging.

Length 8.50, wing 4.50, tail 2.50, tarsus 1, bill .52.

The Quail of the Bahamas differs somewhat from the true *O. virginianus*, but not sufficiently, in my opinion, to characterize it as a variety. The differences do not seem to be greater than would be caused by climatic influences. The inhabitants claim that a number of these birds were imported many years ago from the United States, and have since multiplied so that at the present time they are numerous in the neighborhood of Nassau. Their habits appear to be the same as those of our bird, and they are generally found frequenting the edges of the fields or the open woods, usually in flocks. Their food consists of grain, berries, and occasionally insects. The eggs of this species are pure white.

Fig. Aud. Bds. N. A., Vol. V. pl. 289.

FAM. CHARADRIIDÆ.

THE PLOVERS.

SQUATAROLA HELVETICA. (*Linn.*)

BLACK-BELLIED PLOVER.

Winter Plumage, Male. — Above, dull black, speckled with whitish, barred on the rump; below, grayish white, with more or less dusky on the breast and throat; *axillary plumes, blackish;* it has a small hind toe, hardly noticeable; bill, thick, black.

Length 11, wing 7.30, tail 3.05, tarsus 2, bill 1.10.

The Black-bellied Plover is a regular winter visitant, although it cannot be considered as common. A single specimen was taken on Andros Island in January, and I observed several small flocks during the latter part of the month. They frequent the salt marshes and beaches.

Fig. Aud. Bds. N. A., Vol. V. pl. 315.

CHARADRIUS FULVUS VAR. VIRGINICUS. (Gm.) Borck.

GOLDEN PLOVER.

Adult Male. — Above, speckled with yellowish or grayish; below, white, shaded and mottled with gray; tail, ashy brown, imperfectly barred with gray; *axillary plumes, gray.*

Length 9.10, wing 6.60, tail 2.60, tarsus 1.70, bill .95.

The Golden Plover occasionally visits the Bahamas. Mr. N. B. Moore states that he procured two specimens at Long Island, October 8, the only ones observed by him. On several occasions I observed what I believed to be this species, but was unable to procure a specimen. It frequents the marshes. It may be easily distinguished in any plumage from the preceding by the coloration of the axillary plumes.

Fig. Aud. Bds. N. A., Vol. V. pl. 316.

ÆGIALITIS VOCIFERUS. (Linn.)

KILDEER PLOVER.

Winter Plumage, Male. — Above, dark olive-brown; throat, white, continuing in a band around the neck, edged below with black; narrow upon the back, and broad upon the upper part of the breast, the black band of the breast again succeeded by one of white, shading into the color of the back upon the sides, and that, in turn, by still another band of black reaching to the wings, the feathers of the latter edged with white; forehead, white, the band touching the eyes and succeeded by a black bar across the crown; a superciliary line of tawny white reaching nearly to the nape; under parts, white; rump, orange-brown; tail-feathers, except the central, white (at tips), orange, and black in turn, becoming white again at the base; primaries edged and, except the first two, tipped with white; secondaries, mostly, and coverts tipped with white, forming a bar.

Length 10, wing 6.50, tail 3.80, tarsus 1.50, bill .80.

The Kildeer Plover is an abundant winter visitant, frequenting the fields and marshes. One morning, while shooting upon Norman's Key, I killed a bird of this species, which fell about twenty yards from me; but it had hardly touched the ground before a large Hawk, which I had not before observed, swooped suddenly down upon it, and seized the dead bird in his talons, but upon receiving the contents of my second barrel, which, unfortunately, contained small shot, he dropped the Plover and made off, in a dazed sort of manner, probably very much astonished at his reception.

Dr. Bryant found it very abundant during the winter. Some few birds remain in the Bahamas throughout the year, and probably breed, as I have taken specimens in June in full breeding plumage.

Fig. Aud. Bds. N. A., Vol. V. pl. 317.

ÆGIALITIS WILSONIUS. (Ord.)

WILSON'S PLOVER.

Winter Plumage, Male. — Above, ashy brown; forehead, white, extending into a faint superciliary stripe of dull black on the crown; throat, white, continuing on the sides of the neck, nearly joining upon the nape; a black pectoral band, the feathers edged with white, becoming brown upon the sides; under parts, white; two central tail-feathers, brown, the others showing increasing markings of white to the outer tail-feathers, which are white; bill, black (large and stout); legs, pinkish. Female and immature birds have the pectoral band brown, and no black on the head.

Length 7.45, wing 4.60, tail 1.90, tarsus 1.16, bill .90.

The Wilson's Plover is a resident, and very abundant, generally frequenting the long, open beaches. We found it common on Andros Island, where it was tame and unsuspicious. I also occasionally observed it along the shores of the inland salt ponds. Incubation commences about May 15. On May 27 I procured the eggs of this species near Mathewstown, Inagua. The nest was simply a slight depression in the sand, and contained three eggs, which were quite fresh.

Fig. Aud. Bds. N. A., Vol. V. pl. 319.

ÆGIALITIS SEMIPALMATUS. (Bp.)
RING-NECKED PLOVER.

Adult Male. — Bill short and stout, of an orange-yellow color, tipped with black; legs, yellowish; toes, semipalmate; above, grayish brown, with coronal and pectoral bars of dark brown; eyelids, orange.

Length 6.75, wing 4.50, tail 2.35, tarsus .80, bill .40.

This Plover occasionally visits the islands, but I do not think it is ever at all common. Dr. Bryant, in his list, gives it as "common until May." It is gregarious, and is generally to be found in small flocks frequenting the open beaches.

Fig. Aud. Bds. N. A., Vol. V. pl. 320.

ÆGIALITIS MELODUS. (Ord.)
PIPING PLOVER.

Winter Plumage, Male. — Above, pale ashy brown; throat and band around the neck, white; forehead, white, the color of the back extending upon the side of the breast; under parts wholly white; quills, brown and white; tail, dark brown, with white bases and tips; outer ones, white.

Length 7, wing 4.80, tail 2, tarsus .80, bill .44.

The Piping Plover is abundant throughout the Bahamas during the winter, and I procured specimens as late as June 5, although at that date they were much less common than in winter. I believe that some few remain throughout the year, and of course breed; but I was unable to ascertain this to be a fact. Dr. Bryant gives it as abundant, and "resident throughout the year." It is a social little species, and is generally to be found in flocks frequenting the open beaches.

Fig. Aud. Bds. N. A., Vol. V. pl. 321.

FAM. HÆMATOPODIDÆ.

OYSTER CATCHERS, Etc.

HÆMATOPUS PALLIATUS. Temm.

OYSTER CATCHER.

Local Name. — Sea Pie.

Winter Plumage, Male. — Head and neck blackish or very dark brown; back, brown; lower part of breast and rest of under parts, white; eyelids, rump, tips of wing-coverts, part of secondaries, and basal portion of the tail-feathers, white; bill, orange, darkening at the tip (in summer deep red); legs, flesh-color.

Length 17.40, wing 10.05, tail 4.35, tarsus 2.30, bill 3.50.

The Oyster Catcher is a rather common resident. It may be found frequenting the beaches or small sand-bars, which are exposed at low tide. It was common on Andros Island in January, and very tame. A few were seen at Inagua in June, but I did not succeed in finding its eggs. Dr. Bryant, however, states that it is a resident, and breeds in the Bahamas.

BIRDS OF THE BAHAMA ISLANDS.   151

This species constructs no nest, the eggs being upon the sand in a slight depression made by the scratching of the bird. Two eggs in my cabinet agree with Audubon's description, being of a dull cream-color, spotted with dark brown. This bird is well known to the inhabitants by the name of Sea Pie.

Fig. Aud. Bds. N. A., Vol. V. pl. 324.

STREPSILAS INTERPRES. (*Linn.*)
TURNSTONE.

Winter Plumage, Male. — Above, light, streaked and dashed with dark brown; an imperfect band of dark brown upon the jugulem; chin and upper part of throat, white; sides of breast like the back; rest of the under parts, white; a distinct white band on the wing; rump, white, but with a broad patch of black on the upper tail-coverts; tail, dark brown, the tips and basal half of the inner feathers, and nearly two thirds of the outer feathers, white; legs, reddish orange; bill, black.

Length 8.65, wing 5.70, tail 2.60, tarsus 1, bill .95.

The Turnstone, while passing the winter at the south, becomes a very different looking object from the beautiful bird which we are in the habit of seeing upon our shores during the migrations. He no longer shows the varied colors of his nuptial dress, but becomes as dull colored as the plainest of our Sandpipers. It is abundant in the Bahamas during the winter, frequenting the long, open beaches. A few remain until the latter part of April, and have then begun to assume their harlequin-like costumes once more. Dr. Bryant states that on April 26 he observed a flock on Green Key which were in full spring plumage.

Fig. Aud. Bds. N. A., Vol. V. pl. 323.

FAM. RECURVIROSTRIDÆ.

STILTS, Etc.

HIMANTOPUS NIGRICOLLIS. Vieil.
STILT.

Adult Male. — Top of the head, including the eyes and nape, back, and wings, black; rest of the plumage, white; tail, grayish; legs, pink; bill, black; iris, orange. Immature birds have the upper plumage brownish.

Length 13.50, wing 8, tail 2.70, tarsus 4.20, bill 2.75.

As the summer advances, these birds become very abundant, frequenting the salt ponds and marshes with which these islands abound. At Inagua, almost every pool was tenanted by one or more of them, and during the month of June they were evidently breeding; but although I searched carefully for the nest, I never had the good fortune of finding it. The nest is a rough construction, and generally contains four eggs. While flying the Stilt presents a curious appearance, with its long legs trailing behind it after the manner of the herons. Its note is loud and sharp, and is generally uttered while flying.

Gosse gives an interesting account of this species. He says: "This beautiful and singular bird first fell under my observation in December. It was wading in the water of Crab Pond, picking from the mud at the bottom with the beak, the water reaching not quite half-way up the tarsus. It did not feel with the beak in the manner of the Snipe, but struck at the prey that caught its eye as it walked with the head erect. The statement of Cuvier that walking is painful to the bird, is as contrary to fact as to reason. This specimen was walking in the shallow firmly enough, and even when shot in one leg so as to break it, it stood for some time on the other in a firm, erect attitude, the broken limb being held up and dangling.

"Three were shot at Bluefield's Creek, on the 1st of May, in the evening, out of a large flock that were wading on the little bar at the mouth, and were brought to me. One, which had the wing broken, was alive and otherwise unhurt. It ran actively enough, without the slightest vacillation, taking long strides; but when it was on its belly it could not get on its legs without help, sprawling about with opened wings; it is quite likely, however, that this was owing to one wing being rendered useless, for in attempting to rise, I perceived it always tried to balance by opening and extending horizontally the wings. . . . It frequently stopped abruptly, essayed to go on and stopped again, in that hesitating manner common to the Plovers; and, like them, it often jerked the head up and down. Its usual attitude when standing still was with the neck shortened so that the head projected from between the shoulders, the beak pointing obliquely downwards, and the hinder parts of the body a little elevated. Now and then it lifted one foot, and held it dangling behind the other for a few seconds. Once or twice I saw it pick at the floor, and probably it took a small insect. Its cry, which was uttered once or twice, was a short *clank*, loud, harsh, and abrupt. . . . The stomachs of these contained a few small shells, *Turbo* and *Nerita;* two which Robinson dissected contained 'a kind of *Cornuammonis*,' probably *Planorbis*."

Wilson states that the legs are "exceedingly thin, and so flexible that they may be bent considerably without danger of breaking." In this he is wrong, as the legs, although very slender, are firm and strong.

Fig. Aud. Bds. N. A., Vol. VI. pl. 354.

FAM. SCOLOPACIDÆ.

SNIPES.

GALLINAGO WILSONI. (*Temm.*)

WILSON'S SNIPE.

Winter Plumage, Male. — Bill longer than head; crown, black, with a tawny stripe through the centre; upper parts varied with brownish white, tawny, and black; chin, white; neck and breast, mottled brown and white; feathers of the sides, white, beautifully banded with brown, becoming darker under the wings and very much finer on the flanks; belly, white; primaries tipped with white; crissum streaked with brown and tawny; tail, black, barred with chestnut, black and white at the tip.

Length 11, wing 5.10, tail 2.64, tarsus 1.20, bill 2.50.

During the winter months the Wilson's Snipe becomes abundant in some localities, frequenting marshy ground. Near the Southern Bight, Andros Island, we found them common during the month of January. While walking through marshy spots on many of the other islands we often observed places where they had evidently been boring, but as a rule, but few birds were seen. Like others of its family, it is migratory, and none remain during the summer.

Fig. Aud. Bds. N. A., Vol. V. pl. 350.

MACRORHAMPHUS GRISEUS. (Gm.)

RED-BREASTED SNIPE.

Winter Plumage, Male. — Above, variegated with gray and brown, some of the feathers showing indistinct tawny marks on the wings; throat and upper part of breast, grayish, slightly dotted with brown; sides of the body, under wing-coverts, axillaries, and tail barred with brown and white; belly, white; bill, brownish black; legs, black.

Length 10.75, wing 5.60, tail 2.50, tarsus 1.20, bill 2.48.

On May 27 I procured three birds of this species near Mathewstown, Inagua. They still retained their winter plumage, and were in company with several Sandpipers. They were evidently migrating.

Fig. Aud. Bds. N. A., Vol. VI. pl. 351.

EREUNETES PUSILLUS. (Linn.)

SEMIPALMATED SANDPIPER.

Summer Plumage, Male. — Above, variegated with black, brown, and white; under parts, white, more or less faintly marked with dusky lines on the breast and throat; bill and feet, black. Always easily recognized by its small size and semipalmated toes.

Winter Plumage, Male. — Above mostly ashy gray, showing much white.

Length 6.20, wing 3.80, tail 1.60, tarsus 1, bill 1.10.

This little Sandpiper is a winter resident, and quite abundant. It frequents the open beaches, and is generally met with in flocks. I procured specimens as late as May 27 at Inagua, and observed it upon two occasions afterwards. None were seen after June 5.

Fig. Aud. Bds. N. A., Vol. V. pl. 336.

TRINGA MINUTILLA. *Vieil.*
LEAST SANDPIPER.

Winter Plumage, Male. — Above, ashy gray, streaked and mottled with brown; darkest on the head and back; sides of the head and a band over the upper part of the breast, including part of the throat, pale ash, faintly mottled with brown; upper part of the throat and rest of the under parts, white; primaries and tail, dark brown; a very small species.

Length 5.55, wing 3.40, tail 1.90, tarsus .70, bill .80

This little Sandpiper is one of the most abundant winter visitants. They are very social in disposition, and are generally to be found in large flocks frequenting the open beaches.

Fig. Aud. Bds. N. A., Vol. V. pl. 337.

TRINGA MACULATA. Vieil.

PECTORAL SANDPIPER.

Adult Male. — Bill and feet, greenish; chin, white; breast heavily streaked with gray; upper tail-coverts very dark brown; a large species.

Length 8.25, wing 5.15, tarsus 1.12, bill 1.10.

I include this species on the authority of Mr. N. B. Moore, who states that he procured several specimens at Fortune Island, August 5. I have never met with it in the Bahamas.

Fig. Aud. Bds. N. A., Vol. V. pl. 359.

TRINGA BONAPARTEI. Schl.

WHITE-RUMPED SANDPIPER.

Adult Male. — Bill and feet, black, the former becoming reddish at the base of the lower mandible; above, mottled and streaked with rufous, dark brown, and ashy in summer, ashy and pale brown in winter; below, spotted finely on the breast and throat; belly, white, sides streaked; *rump, white.* The white upper tail coverts are a feature by which it may be easily distinguished.

Length 7.20, wing 4.60, tail 2.40, tarsus .96, bill .96.

The White-rumpled Sandpiper is a regular winter visitant, although not very common. On May 27 I killed two birds of this species in a salt pond near Mathewstown, Inagua. None were observed later.

Fig. Aud. Bds. N. A., Vol. V. pl. 335.

CALIDRIS ARENARIA. (*Linn*)
SANDERLING.

Winter Plumage, Male. — Above, ash and white; under parts, white; tail, except the central feathers, light ash or dull white; primaries with dark edges and tips; secondaries nearly white; bill and feet, black; no hind toe.

Length 7.45, wing 4.50, tail 2.20, tarsus 1, bill .98.

The Sanderling is probably a rather scarce winter visitant. I met with it only once, on January 9, near Hawk Nest, Andros Island, where I procured three specimens. It frequents the beaches and salt marshes.

Fig. Aud. Bds. N. A., Vol. V. pl. 338.

TOTANUS SEMIPALMATUS. *Gm.*
WILLET.

Winter Plumage, Male. — Above, brownish, feathers mottled and barred with brown and dull white; under parts, white, finely barred with brown, almost obsolete on the belly and crissum; axillary plumes, brown; chin and upper part of throat, white; two thirds of primaries, white; tail, white, becoming brownish at the end.

Length 14.50, wing 7.50, tail 2.75, tarsus, 2.25, bill 2.25.

Upon our arrival at Inagua I found this species very abundant, and evidently preparing to breed. Incubation commences about May 15, and at that date they have all repaired to the inland salt ponds. Three or four eggs are deposited on a mat of grass or weeds, slightly raised from the ground. It is interesting to note the curious habit which the Willit has of lighting on the branches of trees. While hunting for the nest I have often seen them perched upon a branch, uttering a short, sharp note, seemingly much agitated at my presence. We found it abundant on many of the islands, especially so at Inagua and Abaco.

Fig. Aud. Bds. N. A., Vol. V. pl. 347.

TOTANUS MELANOLEUCUS. Gm.
GREATER YELLOW-LEG.

Adult Male — Bill, straight; above, ashy, speckled with black and white; below, white, sometimes speckled, and faintly barred with brownish; upper tail-coverts, white, barred with dark brown; tail barred with gray.

Length 12.50, wing 7, tail 3, tarsus 2.56, bill 2.10.

Although not abundant, this well-known species is by no means uncommon during the winter months. Specimens were occasionally taken until June 9, after which none were observed. I never saw more than one or two at a time, and they were always shy. They frequent the open marshes and shores of the salt ponds.

Fig. Aud. Bds. N. A., Vol. V. pl. 345.

TOTANUS FLAVIPES Gm.
YELLOW-LEG.

Adult Male. — Resembles *Melanoleucus*, but is much smaller; coloration almost precisely the same.

Length 11, wing 6.05, tail 2.50, tarsus 1.65, bill 1.70.

This present species is included on the authority of Mr. N. B. Moore, who states that he observed them at Fortune Island and Inagua. I observed two birds which I believed to be of this species, at Bird Rock, Acklin Island.

Fig. Aud. Bds. N. A., Vol. V. pl. 344.

TRINGOIDES MACULARIUS. (Linn.)
SPOTTED SANDPIPER.

Winter Plumage, Male. — Above, olive, becoming slightly brown on the head; feathers of the coverts edged with brown and a very faint line of dull white, showing a slight greenish lustre; carpus mottled with white and brown; throat, ashy, shading into olive on the sides of the breast; a faint superciliary line of dull white touching the eyelid; abdomen and crissum, white; secondaries tipped, and inner primaries spotted with white; lower mandible, greenish, becoming dark at the end.

Length 7.10, wing 3.75, tail 2.05, tarsus .94, bill 1.

The Spotted Sandpiper appears to be a rather scarce resident in the Bahamas. But three specimens were taken,—a solitary individual at Andros Island, Jan. 9, 1879, and two near Bud Rock, Acklin Island, in May of the same year. It is possible that the latter specimens were migrating from some of the more southern islands, and had merely touched at the Bahamas on their way north, in which case it could only be considered as a winter visitant.

Fig. Aud. Bds. N. A., Vol. V. pl. 342.

FAM. TANTALIDÆ.

SPOONBILLS.

PLATALEA AJAJA. Linn.

SPOONBILL.

Adult Male.— Bill spoon-shaped, flat and thin; above, rosy red, whitening towards the neck; lesser wing-coverts, crimson; under parts, pink, whitening on the belly; head, bare, of a greenish color, showing a dark stripe at the base of the skull; tail, orange-brown; legs, pink; feet, black, with touches of pink; iris, red; young birds are grayish white.

Length 26.50, wing 14, tail 5, tarsus 3.50, bill 5.75.

This curious and beautiful species is abundant at Inagua, frequenting the large inland salt lakes which abound on that island. They are very shy, and their breeding-places exceedingly difficult to get at. They are considered excellent eating by the negroes. I had several cooked, and found them quite good, the flesh having a peculiar but not unpleasant flavor. I was told by an old negro, who claimed to have penetrated some distance into the unexplored portions of Inagua, that the Spoonbill was very abundant and tame in some of the small ponds in the interior of the island. The inhabitants say that incubation commences about June 1. Most of the specimens taken during the month of June were in full breeding plumage. The nest is simply a rough construction of sticks, generally built on the mangroves, in which the female deposits two, and according to some writers, three eggs, which are of a dull white color.

Fig. Aud. Bds. N. A., Vol. VI. pl. 362.

FAM. ARDEIDÆ.

HERONS.

ARDEA HERODIAS. Linn.

GREAT BLUE HERON.

Local Name. — Arsnicker.

Adult Male. — Above, grayish blue; neck, grayish brown, with a white line on the throat; head, black, having a white patch on the forehead; below, mostly white and black, sometimes streaked with brown; edge of the wings and feathers of the leg showing orange, brown, and gray; bill, yellow; legs, greenish; iris, yellow.

Length 48, wing 20, tail 7, tarsus 6.50, bill 5.50.

This species is a common winter visitant, and perhaps a resident. During its stay it may be frequently met with on the beaches or in the small inland ponds, but it is extremely watchful and difficult to approach. The flesh of this bird is considered a great delicacy by the inhabitants.

Fig. Aud. Bds. N. A., Vol. VI. pl. 369.

ARDEA EGRETTA. Gm.
GREAT WHITE EGRET.

Winter Plumage, Male. — General color, pure white; *bill and eyes, yellow; feet and legs, black.*

Length 38, wing 16, tarsus 5.80, bill 4.80.

I include the Great White Egret on the authority of Dr. Bryant, who remarks that a "*few were seen.*" I have never met with it in the Bahamas.

Fig. Aud. Bds. N. A., Vol. VI. pl. 370.

ARDEA CANDIDISSIMA. Jacquin.
LITTLE WHITE EGRET.

Adult Male. — Pure white; along occipital a crest of feathers, and also dorsal plumes; bill, black, yellow at the base; legs, *black, yellow behind;* toes, yellow; iris, yellow.

Length 22, wing 11, tarsus 3.50, bill 3.

Dr. Bryant says of this species, that it is more abundant than *Ardea egretta.* I have included it upon his authority.

Fig. Aud. Bds. N. A., Vol. VI. pl. 374.

ARDEA LEUCOGASTRA VAR. LEUCOPRYMNA. (Gm.) (*Licht.*)

LOUISIANA HERON.

Adult Male. — Bill, *black and yellow;* bare space in front of the eye, *yellow;* general plumage, above slaty blue; crest, reddish purple, mixed with dull white; throat, white, mixed with chestnut, heaviest on the lower part, the whole continuing down the front of the neck; under parts, white; under tail-coverts slightly edged with bluish; legs, yellowish green; iris, red.

Length 25, wing 10.50, tail 3.50, tarsus 4, bill 4. (Florida skin.)

I have never taken this bird in the Bahamas, and have therefore included it on the authority of Mr. N. B. Moore, who gives it in his list as occurring on Fortune Island. While on Andros Island during the latter part of January, I observed two birds which I believed to be of this species, but was unable to approach within shot of them.

Fig. Aud. Bds. N. A., Vol. VI. pl. 373.

ARDEA CYANIROSTRIS. Cory.

INAGUA HERON.

Adult Male. — General appearance of the last species. Above, slate-color; crest and base of the neck, purplish, the former mixed with white; throat, white, mixed with reddish brown, narrowing

down the front of the neck; under parts, white; rump, white, concealed by the pale purplish plumes of the back; tail and wings, slaty blue, the outer feathers of the former somewhat pale at the base; more than *terminal* third of *bill* black, the *rest sky blue, shading into* lilac at the base, the latter color extending to the eye; legs, *slate-color;* iris, red.

Length 24, wing 10, tail 3, tarsus 4, bill 4.35.

This species is very nearly allied to *A. leucogastra var. leucoprymna*, the main point of difference between them being in the bill. The plumage of the Bahama bird is also somewhat darker, and the legs and feet slate-color. These features were constant in every specimen taken. That this coloration of the bill is not simply during a high stage of plumage is shown by the fact that Audubon and other writers who found the Louisiana Heron breeding, described the bill as black and yellow. During the summer months these birds were very abundant at Inagua, and upon our arrival in May, we found them breeding in large communities near Roller Key. They were not at all shy, and we procured a large number of specimens, all of which had the same peculiar coloration of the bill. The nest is a rough construction of sticks, generally built within a few feet of the water, and contains from two to four eggs of a pale blue color. None were observed on any of the other islands, although I looked carefully for it everywhere.

ARDEA RUFA. Bodd.
REDDISH EGRET.

Winter Plumage, Male.— Slaty gray; head and neck below, brown; an occipital crest of the same color; lores, flesh-color; iris, white; bill, black on the terminal half, like the lores at the base; legs, bluish. Immature plumage entirely white or slaty gray; legs, greenish; soles of the feet, yellow.

Length 29, wing 14, tail 4, tarsus 5.30, bill 3.90.

There is a great difference in the plumage of young and old birds; some adults are white, while some young birds are colored; but these are exceptions.

The Reddish Egret is a resident, and much more abundant than any other species of its family. Incubation commences about May 15. The nest is a rough structure, composed of sticks loosely put together, and built in the lower branches of the mangroves close to the water. On June 25, I procured two young birds from the same nest, one *pure white* and the other *gray*. Neither of them was then able to fly. The white one appeared to be a weak little thing, and died a few days afterwards; but his brother soon gained strength, grew finely, and is at the present time well and hearty, eats quantities of fish, and amuses itself by chasing stray dogs out of the yard in which it lives.

Fig. Aud. Bds. N. A., Vol. VI. pl. 371.

ARDEA CÆRULEA. Linn.

LITTLE BLUE HERON.

Adult Male.— Slaty blue, shading into purple on the head and neck; bill, blue, becoming dark at the end; legs, black. Immature plumage, pure white, generally showing a tinge of blue usually on the primaries; *legs, greenish blue; toes, yellow.*

Length about 23, wing 11, tarsus 3.60.

The Little Blue Heron is abundant during the winter. All the specimens taken were young birds in the white plumage; no adults were seen. Dr. Bryant regards this bird as "the most common species of Heron. From the nature of the keys, and the general absence of marsh grounds, I had been led to suppose that birds of this family would be rare, but this was by no means the case." None were taken during the summer, although I thought I saw it twice in June.

Fig. Aud. Bds. N. A., Vol. VI. pl. 372.

ARDEA VIRESCENS. Linn.

GREEN HERON.

Winter Plumage. Male.— *An occipital crest of dark green;* neck, chestnut; throat marked heavily with white; under parts pale purplish or ashy, marked with white; back, greenish, showing tinge of slate-color; wing-coverts, green, feathers edged with rufous-white; carpus edged with white; tail, greenish; upper mandible, black; lower mandible, mostly yellow; legs, yellowish green; upper breast-feathers lengthened into a sort of plume, covering a bare space.

Length 16, wing 6.50, tail 2.40, tarsus 1.85, bill 2.30.

An abundant resident, frequenting the marshes and small inland pools. We found them very abundant at Inagua. Incubation commences about May 10. On May 27 I procured a number of their nests, which I found common among the mangroves bordering the inland lake. The nest is roughly constructed of small sticks, loosely put together. The eggs are from three to four in number, of a pale bluish green color.

Gosse, in writing of this species, says, "The flight of all the Herons is flagging and laborious. I have been amused to see a Humming-bird chasing a Heron, — the minuteness and arrowy swiftness of the one contrasting strangely with the expanse of wing and unwieldy motion of the other. The little aggressor appears to restrain his powers in order to annoy his adversary, dodging around him and pecking at him like one of the small frigates of Drake or Frobisher peppering one of the unwieldy galleons of the ill-fated Armada. Now and then, however, I have noticed this and other species of Heron intermit this laborious motion, and sail swiftly and gracefully on balanced wings, particularly when inclining their flight towards the earth. When wounded so as to be unable to fly, the Green Bittern seeks to escape by running, which it does swiftly, the neck projected horizontally, uttering a low cluck at intervals. Its ordinary call, often uttered from the morasses and mangrove swamps, is a loud scream, harsh and guttural. In each specimen that I dissected the stomach was enormous, occupying the whole length and breadth of the body. It usually is found distended with the larvæ of *libelluladæ* and *dyticidæ* and with fresh-water prawns. The latter lie in the stomach always in the same way, viz., doubled up, the head and tail pointing forwards, the only way in which they could be swallowed with safety."

Fig. Aud. Bds. N. A., Vol. VI. pl. 367.

NYCTIARDEA VIOLACEA. (*Linn.*)
YELLOW-CROWNED NIGHT HERON.

Local Name. — Gollden.

Winter Plumage, Male. — Head crested, and plumes of the back reaching beyond the tail; above, bluish gray; feathers of the back, with broad black central stripes; below, showing whitish on the abdomen; head, black, a frontal patch of white with rufous tinge extending into a long crest; above, a shorter one of black; a white stripe on the cheeks; edge of carpus, white; wing-feathers, dark slate, with pale edgings; bill, black; feet, black and yellowish.

Length about 23, wing 13.20, tail 4, tarsus 3.70, bill 2.60.

The Yellow-crowned Night Heron is very abundant throughout the Bahamas. On the desolate little islands of the Miraporvos, we met with them everywhere; dozens of them could be seen at once, standing on the rocks and bushes. On May 27 incubation was already well advanced, but after a careful search I procured a number of eggs in good condition. It builds a rough, flat nest, composed of sticks, generally placed in a low bush, and sometimes several nests were placed in the same bush. The eggs are from three to five in number, of a pale green color. No nest found contained more than that number. The flesh of this bird is much esteemed by the inhabitants of some of the islands.

Fig. Aud. Bds. N. A., Vol. VI. pl. 364.

ARDETTA EXILIS. (Gm.)
LEAST BITTERN.

Adult Male. — Crown, back, and tail, glossy greenish black; back of the neck and some of the wing-coverts, chestnut; the rest of the wing-coverts, yellowish brown; neck and under parts, yellowish brown, varied with white, and showing traces of black on the side of the breast; upper mandible, brown above, below yellow; lower mandible, pale yellow; legs, pale olive-green in front, the rest, including the feet, yellow; iris, pale yellow.

Adult Female. — The black of the upper parts replaced by dark chestnut.

Length 12, wing 4.70, tail 1.65, tarsus 1.65, bill 1.95.

The Least Bittern, although occasionally found in the Bahamas, can only be considered as a rare visitant. A single specimen was taken at Lake Cunningham, New Providence. It frequents marshy ground, and when "flushed" flies but a short distance. According to Audubon, the nest is a flat structure of weed and grass, placed on the ground or in a low bush. It lays from two to five eggs, of a dull white color, sometimes showing a bluish tinge.

Fig. Aud. Bds. N. A., Vol. VI. pl. 366.

FAM. RALLIDÆ.

RAILS, Etc.

RALLUS LONGIROSTRIS. Bodd.
CLAPPER RAIL.

Adult Male.— Above, olive-brown, mottled with gray and ash; a superciliary line and upper throat, whitish; under parts, yellowish brown; flanks and lining of the wing, gray, barred with white; tail, brown.

Length 14.50, wing 5.25, tail 2.10, tarsus 1.85, bill 2.08.

I include this species on the authority of Dr. Bryant, as I have never met with it in the Bahamas. Mr. Arthur Smith observed a large Rail in the neighborhood of Nassau, which may perhaps have been this bird.

Fig. Aud. Bds. N. A., Vol. V. pl. 310.

PORZANA CAROLINA. (*Linn.*)
CAROLINA RAIL.

Winter Plumage, Male.— Above, reddish brown, streaked with black, and some of the feathers edged with white; flanks and lining of the wings barred with white and dull black; abdomen, dull white;

a stripe of black passing from the bill down the centre of the throat, but not reaching the breast; whole of the breast, a cheek patch, and superciliary line, slate-color; crown, chestnut, with a black stripe through the centre; carpus edged with white; crissum, rufous, shading into whitish.

Length 7.75, wing 4.20, tail 2, tarsus 1.38, bill .75.

A regular winter visitant, although by no means abundant. The specimen described above was taken in a small marsh near Long Bay Key, Andros Island, January 13. Two more were seen the following day, and another, a male, was killed January 20.

Fig. Aud. Bds. N. A., Vol. V. pl. 306.

GALLINULA GALEATA. (Licht.)
FLORIDA GALLINULE.

Adult Male. — Head, neck, and under parts, blackish, becoming pale on the belly; back, olive-brown; tail, dusky; flanks striped and wing edged with white; crissum, whitish; bill, with frontal plate, red, sometimes edged with yellowish.

Length 13, wing 6.60, tail 3.10, tarsus 2.

I include this species upon the authority of Dr. Bryant, who claims that it is "abundant and resident the whole year." It cannot be very abundant, for although I looked for it carefully I never met with it on any of the islands.

Fig. Aud. Bds. N. A., Vol. V. pl. 304.

PORPHYRIO MARTINICA. (Linn.)

PURPLE GALLINULE.

Adult Male. — Head, neck, and under parts, bluish purple, grading into black on the belly; above, olive; wing-coverts, bluish; back, olive; crissum, white; frontal plate of the bill, blue; bill, red, tipped with yellow; legs, yellow.

Length 11, wing 6.50, tail 2.65, tarsus 2.30.

Although very desirous of procuring this beautiful bird, I have never had the good fortune of seeing a living specimen. Dr. Bryant was more fortunate, and I include the species on his authority. He says, "I think that this bird must be common; but I met with but one specimen." This Gallinule, as well as the preceding species, frequents the pools and inland ponds, generally preferring fresh water. In Florida this species is much sought after, and its skin commands a high price.

Fig. Aud. Bds. N. A., Vol. V. pl. 303.

FULICA AMERICANA. Gm.

COOT.

Winter Plumage, Male. — Dark slate-color, becoming grayish on the abdomen; head and neck, glossy blue-black; olive markings upon the back; edge of wing and ends of secondaries, white; bill, white, marked with reddish black on the upper, and a spot of the same near the end of the lower mandible; feet, dark olive.

Length 14.75, wing 7.45, tail 2.30, bill, from lower edge of frontal plate, 1.40.

Although some birds of this species remain in the Bahamas through the summer, their numbers are greatly augmented in winter by visitants from the United States. They are very abundant, and at times greatly annoy the sportsman by their incessant clamor as he is making his way through the swamps in search of more desirable game, often frightening away the object of his pursuit long before he has approached within shooting distance. Their flesh is good, and much esteemed by the inhabitants. They are generally found in flocks frequenting the lakes and ponds.

Fig. Aud. Bds. N. A., Vol. V. pl. 305.

FAM. PHŒNICOPTERIDÆ.

FLAMINGOES.

PHŒNICOPTERUS RUBER. (Linn.)

FLAMINGO.

Local Name. — Felimingo.

Adult Male. — Entire plumage, scarlet; most of primaries, black; legs, lake-red; terminal half of bill, black; basal half of lower mandible, orange; young males and females are paler.

Length 52, wing 17, tail 6.50, tarsus 12.50, bill 5.25.

This beautiful species was at one time very abundant throughout the Bahama Islands; but of late years they have been so persecuted by the inhabitants that at the present time they are to be found in any numbers only upon the inland ponds and marshes of Inagua and Abaco. They are gradually dying off, or seeking some more inaccessible locality as yet undisturbed by the presence of mankind, and in all probability with the next century the Flamingo will be unknown in the Bahamas. The inhabitants find their breeding-places and gather hundreds of their eggs. They kill great numbers of the young birds before they are able to fly, and carry

away nearly as many alive to sell to passing vessels, most of which die from want of care. They are killed by hundreds for their feathers, and thus gradually their ranks are being thinned, until at last the Flamingo, like the Dodo and the Solitaire, will be a thing of the past. The nest is a curious structure, composed of clay and mud, and formed somewhat in the shape of a sugar-loaf, with a slight depression on the top, in which they deposit their eggs. At the salt ponds of Inagua and Abaco they still breed in large numbers, but the negroes say that they are becoming fewer and fewer every year. The eggs are white, the shell being covered by a chalky substance. While on the nest, this bird sits with its legs hanging down on either side, and it presents a most ludicrous appearance. I was told by the negroes that Flamingoes are still found on Andros Island.

Fig. Aud. Bds. N. A., Vol. VI. pl. 375.

FAM. ANATIDÆ.

DUCKS.

ANSER HYPERBOREUS. Pall.

Snow Goose.

Adult Male.— Entire plumage, pure white; primaries tipped with black; bill, red. As usually seen, the head shows traces of reddish brown.

Length 29, wing 18, tail 5.50, tarsus 3.20, bill 2.40.

I include the present species provisionally, as the information concerning its occurrence is very meagre. Dr. Bryant states that "he was told by a gentleman that, a few years prior to his visit, a small flock of white or adult birds visited Inagua and were all killed by the inhabitants." He includes it as *Anser cærulescens,* but without doubt, if his information was correct, it should stand as the present species.

Fig. Aud. Bds. N. A., Vol. VI. pl. 381.

DENDROCYGNA ARBOREA. (*Linn.*)

TREE DUCK.

Local Name. — Whistling Duck.

Winter Plumage. — Head, with black band on the crown, continuing in narrow stripes to the nape; forehead and over the eye, reddish brown, shading into dull white on the throat, and mottled brown and white on the sides of the head and neck; breast and upper parts, brown, the feathers broadly edged with tawny; rump and tail, black; under parts, brownish white, heavily spotted and banded upon the sides, the spots becoming very small and faint upon the abdomen; most of the primaries *slate-color*, becoming brownish at the tips; legs and bill, black.

Length 21, wing 11.25, tarsus 2.60, bill 2.

This interesting species is one of the largest of its family. It is a resident, and is not uncommon on some of the larger islands. It generally frequents the inland ponds, which are surrounded by a thick growth of mangroves, and for that reason is not often seen. We found it quite abundant on Andros Island on the ponds situated a few miles from the mouth of Fresh Creek.

ANAS BOSCHAS. *Linn.*

MALLARD.

Adult Male. — Head and neck, glossy green; ring around the lower part of the neck, white; breast, purple-chestnut; wing-coverts tipped with white and black.

Length 24, wing 11.

A very marked species, easily recognized by its large size and green head.

The Mallard is a regular winter visitant, frequenting the inland lakes and ponds. It is a very handsome duck, and is much sought after by sportsmen, as it affords excellent eating. Audubon, in writing of this species says, " The flight of the Mallard is swift, strong, and well sustained. It rises either from the ground or from the water at a single spring, and flies almost perpendicularly for ten or fifteen yards, or if in a thick wood, until quite above the tops of the tallest trees, after which it moves horizontally. If alarmed, it never rises without uttering several *quacks;* but on other occasions it generally leaves its place in silence. While travelling to any distance the whistling sound of their wings may be heard a great way off, more especially in the quiet of the night. Their progress through the air I have thought might be estimated at a mile and a half in the minute; and I feel very confident that when at full speed

and on a long journey they can fly at the rate of a hundred and twenty miles in the hour." Dr. Bryant found this species common during the winter.

Fig. Aud. Bds. N. A., Vol. VI. pl. 385.

DAFILA BAHAMENSIS. (Linn.)
BAHAMA DUCK.

Adult Male. — General plumage, tawny, mottled and streaked with brown; wing, banded with lustrous green, black, and tawny, in the order given; top of head and nape, brown, finely mottled with dark brown, rest of head and throat white; a triangular patch on each side of the upper mandible, lake-red; tail, tawny, becoming pale at the tip; legs, black.

Length 19, wing 8, tail 4.75, tarsus 1.25, bill 1.95.

This pretty little species was quite abundant at Inagua, frequenting the large salt ponds of the interior. On May 27, while shooting on a small island in the lake back of Mathewstown, I observed a number of these birds, and shot several, all of which were in full breeding dress. While passing through a small marsh I discovered the nest of this species, the old bird flying away as I approached. It was simply a mat of grass placed on the ground, and contained nine eggs of a pale brown color. Another nest, taken a few days later, contained eight eggs, slightly darker than the first set.

QUERQUEDULA DISCORS. (Linn.)
BLUE-WINGED TEAL.

Winter Plumage, Male. — Above, dark brown, the feathers edged and streaked with tawny; under parts, pale reddish white, thickly mottled with dull brown spots, showing a tinge of pink on the flanks and lower part of the breast; head, gray, with a purplish tinge; chin and top of the head, velvety black, the latter, bordered by white, joining at the base of the crown and continuing down the nape; a triangular white patch in front of the eye, reaching to the throat; a white patch upon either side of the tail at the base; tail-feathers pointed, dark brown tipped with tawny; wings showing large patches of light blue, metallic green, and white. Female easily recognized by the absence of the white on the head.

Length 15.30, wing 7.05, tail 2.85, tarsus 1.25, bill 1.60.

While exploring Fresh Creek, on Andros Island, in January, I procured a number of these birds in beautiful plumage, scarcely, if ever, equalled by any that I have seen in the United States. They were quite abundant on several of the larger islands, generally being found in flocks frequenting the creeks and ponds. It is only a winter visitant, and none remain to breed.

Fig. Aud. Bds. N. A., Vol. VI. pl. 393.

QUERQUEDULA CAROLINENSIS. (*Gm.*)

GREEN-WINGED TEAL.

Adult Male. — White crescent on the sides of the body just in front of the wings, in some plumages not distinct; a band of green passing from the eye around the base of the skull; *a green wing-band;* under parts mottled on the breast, pale on the belly.

Length about 14, wing 7, tail 3.

According to Dr. Bryant, the Green-winged Teal is common during the winter. I only observed it on two occasions, but there is no doubt that it is a regular winter visitant. I was told by a gentleman, who was well acquainted with the bird, that he had often observed it on Lake Cunningham, near Nassau.

Fig. Aud. Bds. N. A., Vol. VI. pl. 392.

FULIGULA AFFINIS. *Eyton.*

LESSER BLACK-HEADED DUCK.

Adult Male. — Above, grayish, finely streaked with black; head, black, showing greenish gloss; bill, dull blue, tipped with black.

Adult Female. — Easily distinguished from the male by having the face whitish.

Length 17, wing 8.50.

As soon as the cold weather sets in, the Lesser Black-headed Duck appears in our Southern waters. Many of them visit the Bahamas during January and February, and become abundant in the lakes and ponds. Dr. Bryant found it common during the winter, and included it in his list as *Felix marila* (*Fuligula marila*), but if *F. affinis* is distinct from *F. marila*, those found in the Bahamas should stand as the former species.

Fig. Aud. Bds. N. A., Vol. VI. pl. 397.

FULIGULA COLLARIS. (*Donovan*.)
RING-NECKED DUCK.

Adult Male. — Bill, bluish black, pale at the base, and a band near the tip; head, breast, and upper parts, dull black, showing slight greenish reflection on the back; below, white, finely mottled with gray on the sides; a reddish brown ring forming a collar around the neck. In winter the under parts are often marked with gray, the back somewhat brownish, and the ring on the neck showing a yellowish tinge. Female with head and neck brownish, the collar wanting.

Length 17, wing 8, bill 2.

This species is abundant in the Bahamas during the winter. It was occasionally seen, generally in flocks, in company with other species of its family.

Fig. Aud. Bds. N. A., Vol. VI. pl. 398.

FULIGULA FERINA VAR. AMERICANA. (*Linn.*) *Coues.*

RED-HEADED DUCK.

Adult Male. — Bill, dull blue, black at the end; head and neck, reddish brown; crown of the head, dark; a broad black collar covering the upper breast and upper back; back, grayish, delicately lined with brown, so fine as to be almost indistinct; under parts, white, showing a tinge of gray; rump, black.

Length 19, wing 9.50.

The present species is a winter visitant. It was abundant on the inland lakes of the island of New Providence in January, and ranges throughout the Bahamas wherever it can find suitable feeding-grounds. Its flesh is much esteemed as an article of food.

Fig. Aud. Bds. N. A., Vol. VI. pl. 396.

ERISMATURA RUBIDA. (*Wils.*)

RUDDY DUCK.

Adult Male, Fall Plumage. — Above, brown, streaked with dusky; below, brownish, with a tawny tinge; crown and nape, dark brown; crissum, white.

Length 15.50, wing 5.05, tarsus 1.20.

The Ruddy Duck is a common winter visitant. During my stay they were abundant in December and January on Lake Cunningham and Miller's Pond, in the neighborhood of Nassau, but all had left as soon as spring had fairly set in. This species is a very expert diver, and will often plunge beneath the surface and swim under water until it has concealed itself among the reeds near the shore, in preference to taking flight at the approach of some enemy.

Fig. Aud. Bds. N. A., Vol. VI. pl. 399.

FAM. SULIDÆ.

GANNETS.

SULA FIBER. (*Linn.*)

BOOBY GANNET.

Adult Male.—Head, throat, upper part of breast, tail, and entire upper plumage, dark olive-brown; under parts, white; gular sack, pale yellow; upper mandible, greenish; feet, pale yellowish green; iris, yellowish.

Length 27, wing 15.50, tail 8, tarsus 1.60, bill 4.

About the 1st of February this species repairs to the desolate and uninhabited keys to breed. At the Miraporvos we procured a number of the old birds as well as a few fully fledged young ones, but they were evidently preparing to leave. Dr. Bryant gives an interesting account of an earlier visit to these breeding-grounds. He says, "My first visit to one of their breeding-places was made on the 10th of April, at St. Domingo Key, which lies thirty-three miles south of Great Ragged Island, and is at the very extremity of the southern point of the bank, entirely out of the range of vessels of any kind, and is probably never visited except occasionally by people from Ragged Island, who go there to collect the eggs of the Noddy. The key is about three or four acres in extent, so low that in storms it is entirely washed by the waves. It can only be approached at one spot, and that only at calm weather. At the time of my visit, it was literally covered with Boobies, mostly young ones. Of these, by far the greater part were fully fledged, and could fly with ease, but were still dependent on the parent birds for food. They kept by themselves, and were perched upon the rocks all around the edge of the key. The younger birds were sprinkled all over the key, wherever there was room for them, and of all ages, from those almost able to fly, to young ones but that moment hatched. I found the eggs of some twenty pairs, most of them on the point of hatching. The number in every case was two, though only one is usually attributed to them. In appearance, they resemble those of the family generally, being greenish, covered with a chalky substance; in size they vary considerably, as also in form. The most elongated one measured 0.67 in length by 0.38 in breadth, and the broadest 0.55 by 0.40, the others varying between these two extremes, but averaging more nearly the latter. The young, when first hatched, are entirely naked, and of a livid blue color. They soon become covered with a white down, then the quills and tail-feathers make their appearance, of a cinereous brownish color, then the feathers of the body, neck, and head, and, lastly, of the throat.

"On our landing, some of the old birds flew off, but by far the greater number remained, and did not trouble themselves to get out of our way, but on being approached too near, darted at us with their powerful bills in a most savage manner. They seemed to be very quarrelsome in their disposition, continually striking at each other, not at all in an amicable manner, but as if they intended to do all the mischief in their power. How the different birds recognized their young was a mystery to me, as they apparently did not remain in the same place after they had attained any size.

"Besides St. Domingo Key, I visited a number of other breeding-places, all of which resembled the one described, except in being more elevated above the water. The Booby is, I think, the most expert diver that I am acquainted with; no matter in what position it may be, whether flying in a straight line, sailing in a circle, just rising from the water, or swimming on the surface, the instant it sees its prey it plunges after it. I have frequently seen one dive from the wing, rise to the surface, and dive in rapid succession five or six times; and on taking flight again, dive before it had risen more than two or three feet from the surface, and perhaps catch a dozen fish in the space of a minute. There is nothing graceful in its style; it is apparently work and not pleasure.

"On one of the keys I visited, called Booby Key, near Green Key, I saw a great number of a species of Anolis, of a dark, almost black color, entirely unlike any seen elsewhere, but they were so timid and active in their movements that I could not procure a specimen. The stomach contained a great many varieties of fish; among them a cottus, a parrot-fish, flatfish of two species, and some large prawns; but their principal food seemed to be flying-fish and a species of hemirhamphus."

Fig. Aud. Bds. N. A., Vol. VII. pl. 426.

SULA DACTYLATRA. (*Lesson.*)

I append Dr. Bryant's description and account of this species, as I have never met with it.

Description. — "Sexes similar; form more robust than that of the *S. fiber;* secondaries and tertiaries, rich brown, the primaries of the same color, but darker; some of the coverts of the primaries brownish; tail, with the feathers below, brown, above, hoary, the two middle feathers the most so, and the base of all white or whitish; all the rest of the plumage snowy white; bill, horn-color, with the serrations of the upper mandible very distinctly marked; iris, pale yellow; naked skin around the bill; eyes and throat, black; tarsi and feet, yellowish green.

"Lesson's description of this bird is not sufficiently full to enable me to decide with certainty whether it is the same as those I procured at the Bahamas. If it should prove to be a new species, the name *elegans* would be appropriate, as it is the prettiest of the genus. In dimensions, it is about the size of the *Sula fusca,* but heavier and more muscular. I found them breeding but at one place, St. Domingo Key, and there some twenty pairs. They apparently lay their eggs later than the Booby, as the largest of the young were not more than half grown, and the eggs of several were freshly laid. They were whiter than those of the latter bird, the chalky covering being much thicker, and did not differ as much in size or proportions. They did not associate with the other species; the young birds and eggs were all in one part of the island. When half fledged, they are very pretty, the snowy-white down with which they are covered forming a striking contrast with the dark brown of the tail and wings just appearing. Their habits are just the same as those of the Boobies, and their internal structure presents no appreciable difference."

FAM. PELECANIDÆ.

PELICANS.

PELECANUS FUSCUS. Linn.
BROWN PELICAN.

Winter Plumage, Male. — Sack, dark purple. Above, slate-color and dark brown variegated; neck of the adult, reddish brown; head, mostly white; bill, darker, marked with red; feet, purplish black; iris, yellowish. Females generally have the neck yellowish white.

Length 53, wing 18, tail 7.40, tarsus 2.50, bill 10.

The present species is abundant throughout the Bahamas, where it is a resident, and breeds in great numbers on some of the islands. While paddling among the mangroves, I often observed it sitting upright on the half-sunken branches, or floating silently with the tide, watching keenly for any fish that might come within reach of its long beak, which it uses with great dexterity.

Incubation commences the latter part of January; the nest, which is very roughly constructed, is generally built on the mangroves. Dr. Bryant found it very abundant. He says, " At the Biminis, the Brown Pelican was numerous, and breeding on the mangroves in the same manner as in Florida. On the 20th of February, the young were hatched in some of the nests, and incubation was advanced in all of them. I did not meet with the bird anywhere else. The development of the air-cells is greater in this bird than in any other that I am acquainted with. On touching it while alive, a distinct crepitus is felt and heard, and as if it were emphysematous; all the bones, with the exception of the phalanges of the toes, contain air. It possesses much more intelligence than I gave it credit for. A tame one, belonging to the Colonel of Engineers at Nassau, was in the habit of going every morning to the fish market. Fish are always sold alive, and in order that the purchaser may select them, are taken out of the water and spread before him; this was the moment for the Pelican, and if he had been as active as he was voracious, he would have fared well; but unfortunately for him, the fishermen were generally too quick, and, seizing him by his long beak, would throw him into the water, where he would remain for some time, looking with great solemnity at his persecutors, and then return to try his luck again. As I was passing by his owner's house one day, he commenced tugging at my trousers with his bill; at first I did not understand what he wanted, but noticing that the gate was shut, thought it possible that he might wish it opened; this I accordingly did, and he walked in at once, without stopping to thank me. This bird was in immature plumage, probably not more than a year old."

FAM. GRACULIDÆ.

CORMORANTS.

GRACULUS DILOPHUS VAR. FLORIDANUS. (*Sw.*) (*Aud.*)

FLORIDA CORMORANT.

Winter Plumage, Male. — Smaller than *C. carbo*, but bill about as large; above, greenish black; feathers of the back and coverts, gray, edged with dark brown; head and neck, dark brown, shading into grayish on the throat, and dull white mottled with pale brown below; rump, tail, and feet, black; sac and lores, bright yellow.

Length 29.50, wing 11.50, tail 6, tarsus 2, bill 2.05.

An abundant species. On Jan. 18, 1879, while exploring Fresh Creek, Andros Island, a pair of young birds of this species were captured. They were but a few weeks old and not able to fly, so that after an exciting scramble through the bushes we caught them, and packed them away snugly in the bow of the boat. The nest was built in a clump of mangroves, about fifteen feet from the water, and was merely a mass of small sticks and grass, loosely thrown together.

The young birds were at first very savage, and although they could not really injure any one, their little sharp bills cut the skin as easily as a knife. Signs of this bad disposition continued for some days, but gradually they seemed to become accustomed to civilized life, and became quite affectionate, running in an ungainly manner towards me whenever I appeared with a fish in my hand. It was amusing to watch the struggles of the youngsters in their endeavors to swallow fish nearly as large as themselves, and their apparent disgust at being unsuccessful. After a while a tub half full of water was placed at their disposal, in which they splashed about, seeming to enjoy it greatly. About two months after their capture, the smaller bird seemed to grow gradually weaker and weaker, and one morning we found him lying dead in his box. The other seemed to mope for a few days after the loss of his brother, but soon recovered his spirits and became as lively as ever. As he grew older he became more and more difficult to please in regard to his food. Nothing would tempt him to eat a fish which had been dead over night. Oftentimes while cruising from one island to another we were detained by contrary winds and unable to procure fresh fish with which to feed him. At such times he would eat nothing, and it was necessary to force food down his throat to keep him from starving. When very hungry or teased by one of the men, he would walk around the deck with his mouth open, uttering a peculiar guttural sound. Incubation commences about December 10.

Fig. Aud. Bds. N. A., Vol. VI. pl. 417.

FAM. TACHYPETIDÆ.

TACHYPETES AQUILUS. (*Linn.*)

MAN-OF-WAR BIRD.

Adult Male. — Entire plumage, brownish black, showing a greenish reflection on the head, and purplish upon the back; tail forked, and composed of twelve feathers; gular sac, pale orange; iris, brown.

Adult Female. — Differs from the male by having a white patch on the breast, passing along the sides of the neck, and around near the middle.

Length 43, wing 25, tail 19, tarsus 1, bill 6.

The "Frigate," as it is sometimes called, frequents all of the Bahama Islands, but only during the breeding season do they appear to congregate in any one place. They remain throughout the year, but seem to become more numerous as the Terns commence to arrive. While at Abaco, on June 24, we procured a number of nests, containing young birds apparently between two and three weeks old. The nest was placed in mangrove-bushes close to the water's edge. For the first few days the young birds would not eat anything, and it was necessary to force food down their throats to keep them alive; but after a time they began to eat of their own accord, and after that we had no further trouble with them otherwise than to furnish them with sufficient food, which it was not always easy to do. Upon being approached, they snapped their bills loudly, at the same time uttering a sharp whistling noise.

Dr. Bryant gives an interesting account of their breeding habits. He says, " I found a few Man-of-War Birds breeding at the Biminis; their nests were placed upon the mangroves, amidst those of the Brown Pelican and Florida Cormorant. As these birds are much disturbed by the inhabitants, their breeding-places will probably be given up in a few years. On the central and highest part of Booby Key, a colony of about two hundred pairs was breeding. The nests here were on the bare rock, and closely grouped together, the whole not occupying a space more than forty feet square. There were no Boobies amongst them, though thousands were breeding on the key. The largest breeding-place visited by me is situated on Seal Island, one of the Ragged Island keys, and is five or six acres in extent. The nests, thickly crowded together, were placed on the tops of prickly-pear, which covered the ground with an almost impenetrable thicket. On the 8th of April the young were hatched in half of the nests, the largest about one third grown; the other nests contained eggs more or less hatched. Out of many hundreds, I procured only seven that were freshly laid.

" I have visited the breeding-places of many sea birds before, and some well worth the trouble, but none so interesting to me as this.

It was a most singular spectacle: thousands and thousands of these great, and ordinarily wild birds, covered the whole surface of the prickly-pears as they sat on their nests, or darkened the air as they hovered over them, so tame that they would hardly move on being touched; indeed, the specimens that I procured were all taken alive, with my own hands. When I had penetrated as far among them as possible, I fired my gun; the whole colony rose at once, and the noise made by their long and powerful wings striking against each other was almost deafening. In a moment they commenced settling upon their nests, and were soon as quiet as before. Incubation is carried on by both male and female. The old ones feed the young at first by regurgitation. The food consists of the same species of fish as the Booby's, and is principally derived from that bird, whom they rob as the Bald Eagle does the Fish Hawk. Why the Booby should submit to this, being much more powerful and armed with a most formidable bill, is strange. I have watched these birds for hours while flying, and every now and then hovering over the surface of the water, but never saw them catch a fish. The popular idea at the Bahamas is, that the fish are stupefied by the excrement of this bird. If there is any foundation for this idea, I presume it is that the fish are attracted by it; though the abundance of fish is such, that one would think it hardly worth while to attract them in any way.

"The young are at first nearly naked, then covered with a white down, and by the time they are the size of a Pigeon have the bronzed black scapulars so developed that they look, whilst sitting on their nests, erect on the tarsi, as if they had on cloaks. They were not quarrelsome in their disposition, like the Boobies; frequently one would alight on a neighboring nest without being disturbed by the owner. The single egg, which is white, is large for the size of the body."

Although the Man-of-War is quite tame during the breeding season, at other times it is shy and suspicious and very difficult to approach. We met with them every day among the more southern islands, and one or more of them was generally to be seen, but they generally gave the vessel a wide berth, and it was a rare thing to obtain a shot at one of them. The young birds, when about three weeks old, are pure white, with the exception of a slight tinge of blackish upon the back, the bill and gular sac at that time being pale flesh-color.

Fig. Aud. Bds. N. A., Vol. VII. pl. 421.

FAM. PHAETHONTIDÆ.

TROPIC BIRDS.

PHAETHON FLAVIROSTRIS. Brandt.

TROPIC BIRD.

Local Name. — Egg Bird.

Adult Male. — Bill, pale orange-yellow; general plumage, white, sometimes slightly rosy-tinted; most of primaries showing much black, a streak passing through the eye; some of the wing-coverts and shafts of tail-feathers, black; tail extended into two very long feathers, which are reddened; tarsus, bluish; iris, black; webs and toes, black.

Length, including tail-feathers, 31.50, wing 11, tail 21, tarsus .90, bill 2.

This elegant and graceful species becomes abundant among the Bahamas during the summer months. They are never found breeding together in large communities, like the *Anous stolidus* or *Sterna fuliginosa*, but appear to be more solitary in their habits.

Dr. Bryant, in writing of this species, says, "I visited three breeding-places at Long Rock, near Exuma. They breed in holes in the horizontal surface of the rock, as also at Water Key, one of the Ragged Island keys. At Key Verde, which is situated about thirty miles east of Great Ragged Island, in holes in the perpendicular face of the cliffs, and also in the horizontal surface of the rock. Before depositing their eggs, the male and female occupy the same hole, but afterwards only one bird is found in the hole. Both sexes incubate. On the 20th of April about half of the birds had not commenced laying, and a few of the eggs had been sat on for three or four days; most of them, however, were freshly laid. They feed from near daylight to about nine o'clock, when they return to their holes, in which they pass the hotter part of the day, again leaving them toward sunset in search of food. They cannot, of course, breed in communities like the Tern, as suitable holes are not very abundant. At Water Key, where they were more abundant than at any other place, in an extent of two miles, only eleven birds were found. The holes chosen for their abodes are seldom shallow, and are often so winding that, though their harsh note can be heard, they can only be procured by demolishing the rock.

"In their habits, except that of diving, which I am ignorant whether they practise or not, they closely resemble the Terns, as they also do in their mode of flight and external appearance; and with that family they should be associated. On their breeding-places being approached, when they are out of their holes, they hover over the intruder, screaming, and darting at him in precisely the same manner that the Terns do. The long tail-feathers are never separated when flying, and the French name, *paille en queue*, is very expressive. I procured a single specimen, with a pale straw-colored bill; it was a male, the plumage nearly pure white, much more so than in any of the orange-billed birds, and the fifth primary had the black narrowly edged externally with white the whole length. I am not prepared to say that this bird, which agrees with the exceptions above mentioned, with the other, is a different species, and if so, which of them is the Flavirostris of Brandt. The orange-billed specimens were both male and female, and there was no external peculiarity by which the sex could be determined.

"The figure in Gray's 'Genera' of this bird is very good. My specimen agrees generally with Mr. George W. Lawrence's description in the ninth volume of the Pacific Railroad Report. They are precisely alike in their markings, varying only in the shade of salmon, which is always deepest on the long tail-feathers, and next on the back and hind neck. The tarsus and hind toe are not yellow, but flesh-colored, and this color extends obliquely across the foot from the basal extremity of the outer toe to the end of the first phalange of the inner toe. There is no black that I can discover at the base of the sixth primary, though its shaft, as well as those of all the others, is black, except toward the tip. The white tips of the five outer primaries diminish in extent from the first to the third, and then again increase to the fifth. The single egg is large for the size of the bird, whitish, covered almost entirely with reddish chocolate-colored spots, finely dotted over the surface, which can be easily rubbed off. The small number that I procured were of nearly the same form and dimensions. One of them measured .053 in length by .042 in breadth; in shape, very similar to a common hen's egg. The eggs were sometimes deposited upon the bare rock and sometimes on a few twigs, which had, however, the appearance of having accidentally fallen into the hole."

The flight of this graceful species does not at all resemble the long, easy movements of the Gulls, but is hurried and rapid, more resembling that of a Duck. As a rule, they appeared to be rather shy, and it was an unusual thing for us to obtain a shot at one of them while coasting along the shores of the islands; although they were often seen, they seldom approached within shooting distance of the vessel. The inhabitants call them Egg Birds, and prefer their eggs as an article of food to those of the Terns or Gulls.

Fig. Aud. Bds. N. A., Vol. VII. pl. 427.

FAM. LARIDÆ.

GULLS, TERNS.

LARUS ATRICILLA. Linn.

LAUGHING GULL.

Adult Male. — Bill, lake red; hood, grayish black; nape, white, forming a sort of collar; upper parts, pearl-gray; beneath, white; outer primaries, dark brown; tail, white; feet, black, with red on the webs; iris, dark brown.

Length 15.50, wing 12.50, tail 5, tarsus 1.90, bill 1.40.

About the time that the visitors who have been spending the winter at Nassau begin to leave for the north, the Laughing Gull appears, and may be daily seen passing in and out among the numerous vessels anchored in the harbor. We found it abundant throughout the whole of the Bahamas after April, and at Inagua it was evidently breeding, although our search for its eggs proved unsuccessful.

Fig. Aud. Bds. N. A., Vol. VII. pl. 443.

LARUS PHILADELPHIA. (Ord.)

BONAPARTE'S GULL.

Winter Plumage, Male. — Above, pearly blue; under parts, white; a spot of black on the side of the base of the skull; first four primaries mostly white, tipped with black, which in turn is tipped with white on the third and fourth; nearly the whole of the outer web of the first primary, black; feet, yellow, tinged with red; webs, vermilion. Immature birds have a band of dark brown on the tail.

Length 12.50, wing 9.75, tarsus 1.30, bill 1.15.

I include this species on the authority of Mr. N. B. Moore, who says that he closely observed a bird of this species at Long Island, October 8. I have never met with it, but there is no reason why it should not occasionally visit the Bahamas, as it is common on the Florida coast in winter.

Fig. Aud. Bds. N. A., Vol. VII. pl. 442.

STERNA ANGLICA. Montagu.

GULL-BILLED TERN.

Adult Male. — Bill, black, short and stout; cap, black; above, pearl-gray; under parts, white; first two primaries tipped with brown; tail forked; legs, black; iris, brown.

Length 13, wing 11.75, tail 5, tarsus 1.10, bill 1.32.

On most of the southern islands, the Gull-billed Tern becomes common during the summer months. It is a curious fact that this bird was not observed by Dr. Bryant during his visits, as it is one of the most abundant species of its genus at Inagua, where, in the month of June, it was evidently breeding.

Fig. Aud. Bds. N. A., Vol. VII. pl. 430.

STERNA REGIA. Gambel.

ROYAL TERN.

Adult Male. — Bill, orange, reddish at the base; above, pearl gray; primaries showing much white on the inner webs; crown, black, the feathers extending in a sort of crest to the back; below, white; tail, white and forked.

Length 19, wing 14.50, tail 7.50, tarsus 1.25, bill 2.25.

The Royal Tern is abundant throughout the Bahamas. It is distinguished by its large size from any of the other Terns which frequent the islands. The young bird has the bill pale orange, without any traces of red, and the plumage is somewhat spotted. During the winter the crown of the adult bird becomes mixed with white and the color of the bill somewhat paler. None were observed later than May.

STERNA CANTIACA. (Gm.)
SANDWICH TERN.

Spring Plumage, Male. — Bill, black, tipped with yellow; cap, black; upper back, whitish, rest of upper plumage, pearl-gray; under parts, white, sometimes tinged with rose; first primary edged with white to the tip, covering the entire inner web at the base, and narrowing to an almost imperceptible line at the tip; tail, white, forked; legs, black; iris, dark brown.

Length 14, wing 10.50, tail 4.40, tarsus .90, bill 1.90.

This interesting species is occasionally found in summer. At Bird Rock, Acklin Island, they were quite abundant during the latter part of May, and were evidently preparing to breed, although we were unable to find their eggs. Their flight is strong and very graceful, and they dive and fish with great dexterity.

Fig. Aud. Bds. N. A., Vol. VII. pl. 431.

STERNA HIRUNDO. Linn.
COMMON TERN.

Adult Male. — Bill, red, becoming black on the terminal third; cap, black; above, pearl-blue; under parts, white, washed with plumbeous, scarcely showing on the throat; tail mostly white; outer web of the outer tail-feathers darker than the inner web; feet, red. In the young bird the cap is imperfect; the under parts are pure white, and the bill is often black.

Length 13.75, wing 10, tail 6, tarsus .75, bill 1.38.

Dr. Bryant included this species in his list as abundant, but as he did not find *S. paradisæa*, it is probable that many of the birds seen by him, supposed to be the Common Tern, were of the latter species. The Common Tern is probably rather uncommon in the Bahamas. I observed it only once, a single specimen shot at Acklin Island in May.

Fig. Aud. Bds. N. A., Vol. VII. pl. 433.

STERNA PARADISÆA, Brunn.

ROSEATE TERN.

Adult Male. — *Bill slender, black;* cap, black, reaching the nape; upper plumage, pearl-gray; under parts, pinkish white, in the full plumage adult becoming a beautiful rose-color; *the white of the inner web of the first primary reaching the tip;* tail, white, two outer feathers much longer than the rest; legs, vermilion-red; iris, brown. Younger birds have the base of the bill colored.

Length 15, wing 9, tail 7.50, tarsus .80, bill 1.60.

The beautiful Roseate Tern, although by no means abundant, is a regular summer visitant. A few specimens in full breeding dress were taken at Acklin Island during the latter part of May, and we found them common at Clarence Harbor, Long Island, in June, nearly always in company with Sandwich or Sooty Terns. The eggs are simply deposited on the sand, without any nest whatever, as is usual with birds of this genus. The beautiful rose-color of the breast fades soon after the bird dies, either becoming pale or disappearing altogether.

Fig. Aud. Bds. N. A., Vol. VII. pl. 437.

STERNA SUPERCILIARIS. *Vieil.*

LEAST TERN.

Adult Male.— Bill, yellow, tipped with black; cap, black; forehead, white; above, pearly gray; under parts, white; outer primaries, dark brown on outer webs and inner half of inner webs; tail, white, forked; coverts, pearl-gray; legs, pale yellow; iris, brown.

Length 8.75, wing 6.50, tail 2.20, tarsus .55, bill 1.

In summer the Least Tern becomes rather common on most of the southern islands. During the latter part of May they were quite abundant at Inagua. At this time most of them had repaired to the inland salt ponds, and incubation had already commenced.

On June 2 I found several large flocks of them breeding together, and procured a number of their eggs, many of which contained large embryos. The eggs were deposited in a slight depression in the sand. The female lays from one to two eggs, and I have never found over that number, although it has been claimed by some writers that three are often found.

Fig. Aud. Bds. N. A., Vol. VII. pl. 439.

STERNA FULIGINOSA. Gm.

Sooty Tern.

Adult Male. — Bill, black; crown and entire upper plumage, black; forehead, white, extending into a pair of horns, *not reaching above the eye;* under parts, white; outer tail-feathers, white, showing very dark brown for about two inches on the inner webs near the tip; legs, black; iris, brown.

Length 16.50, wing 11.50, tail 7, bill 1.60, tarsus .90.

The uninhabited reefs and small islands are frequented every spring by innumerable quantities of these birds, which find there a secure retreat in which to rear their young, undisturbed by man. At the Miraporvos whole islands are covered with them. As a rule they deposit their eggs in some cleft in the rocks or beneath the shelter of some cactus-bush. The nest is simply a mat of grass

roughly put together, on which a single egg is laid; sometimes the egg is deposited upon the bare rock, without any pretensions to a nest whatever. They appear to live in perfect harmony with the Noddy Terns, which also breed in great numbers upon this island. Incubation commences about May 16. On the 23d, all the eggs obtained were quite fresh.

Fig. Aud. Bds. N. A., Vol. VII. pl. 432.

STERNA ANOSTHÆTA. *Scopoli.*

BRIDLED TERN.

Spring Plumage, Male.—Bill, black; cap, black; forehead, white, *extending like two horns over each eye, and reaching behind them;* upper back, grayish, shading into the white on the sides of the neck; upper plumage, grayish brown; under parts, white; primaries, dark brown, the first and second showing a clear band of white on the inner webs, not reaching within an inch of the tips, and gradually fading on the others; upper tail-coverts, slaty gray; outer tail-feathers *almost entirely white*, showing slight tinge of brownish near the tip; legs and feet, black; iris, brown.

Length 14.25, wing 10, tail 6.25, tarsus .70, bill 1.50.

I was very much pleased to find this species abundant at Long Island during the month of June. Its occurrence on the Florida coast has been a question of dispute for some time, but can now no longer be doubted, as the near proximity of Long Island to Florida would render its occurrence on our coast more than likely. In all probability it is a regular summer visitant to our southeastern shores. Upon our arrival at Clarence Harbor we found it abundant, and breeding in company with the Sooty and the Roseate Terns. Until June 8 all the eggs which we found were quite fresh.

In breeding habits the Bridled and the Sooty Terns resemble each other. When about to lay, the female selects a sheltered cleft in some ledge, or a cavity among the loose rocks along the shore, and there deposits a single egg, which is slightly larger than that of the Sooty Tern, and has a faint reddish tinge.

ANOUS STOLIDUS. (Linn.)
NODDY TERN.

Adult Male. — Bill, black; forehead, white, shading into gray at the base of the skull; lower eyelid, white; front of the eye and narrow superciliary line, blackish; entire plumage, rich olive-brown; primaries, dark brown, the first having the inner web pale brown; legs, black; iris, dark brown.

Length 15, wing 10, tail 5.75, tarsus .80, bill 1.70.

During the summer months these birds repair in immense quantities to the uninhabited reefs and small islands to breed. At the Miraporvos the islands were covered with them. Upon landing we were at once surrounded by an innumerable quantity of these birds, circling around us, uttering incessant cries, as if trying to drive us away from their nests, which we could see on all sides of us. At this spot we could have gathered many barrels of eggs had we wished to do so, for there seemed to be no limit to them. The nests are composed of grass and sticks, and are generally built upon the low cactus-bushes with which the whole island is covered. Occasionally an egg was found simply deposited upon the rock. Incubation commences about the latter part of May. On May 23 all the eggs collected were quite fresh.

Fig. Aud. Bds. N. A., Vol. VII. pl. 440.

FAM. PROCELLARIIDÆ.

PETRELS.

OCEANITES OCEANICA. (Kuhl.)
WILSON'S PETREL.

Adult Male. — Entire plumage, dark brown; wing-coverts edged with whitish brown; upper tail-coverts, white; tail, black; bill, black; toes with yellow spots on the webs; iris, brown.

Length 7, wing 5.64, tail 2.45, tarsus 1.25, bill .60.

The Wilson's Petrel becomes abundant a short distance off the coast, but I have never observed it very near the land. While cruising among the islands, numbers of these Petrels followed in the wake of the vessel, only leaving us upon our near approach to the shore.

Fig. Aud. Bds. N. A., Vol. VII. pl. 460.

PUFFINUS MAJOR. Faber.
GREATER SHEARWATER.

Adult Male. — Dark brown, somewhat grayish on the head; upper tail-coverts mostly white; below, white; lining of wings, white; tail, dark brown; crissum, dark; front of tarsi, dark, the rest pale.

Length 18, wing 13, tail 5.75, tarsus 2, bill 2.40.

I have never taken this Shearwater in the Bahamas, but on several occasions saw what I believed to be this species while cruising among the islands.

Fig. Aud. Bds. N. A., Vol. VII. pl. 456.

PUFFINUS OBSCURUS. (Gm.)

DUSKY SHEARWATER.

Local Name. — Pimblico.

Adult Male. — Above, glossy brown, shading into grayish upon the sides of the breast; below, white; crissum, brown and white; tail, brown, the feathers faintly tipped with ashy; bill, lead-color.

Length 12.50, wing 8, tail 4.25, tarsus 1.60, bill 1.30.

The Dusky Shearwater is an abundant resident, but, from its peculiar habits, is sometimes quite difficult to procure. They are very shy, and remain far out at sea during the day, only returning to the land after it has become too dark to be able to distinguish them. All night long their mournful cries can be heard, but long before dawn they are off again, and a search with the hope of finding any near the shore would be useless. We often observed them in large flocks when out of sight of land, seeming to be quietly resting on the water, but it was a rare thing for them to allow us to approach near enough to obtain a shot from the vessel. Dr. Bryant gives an interesting account of this species, which I quote in full, as, unfortunately, I did not visit any of their breeding-places during the period of incubation, and am therefore unable to state anything regarding their breeding habits from personal experience. He says:—

"On making inquiries as to what sea birds breed on the keys, I was constantly told of a singular bird, with a hooked bill, that only flew during the night, and was known by the name of Pimblico. It proved to be the present species. It is very abundant, being found on all the uninhabited keys near the channel which are not too frequently visited by wreckers or fishermen. They breed in holes in the rocks, as described in the 'Naturalist in Bermuda.' Near Nassau, at the Ship Channel Keys, where I first met with them, incubation had already commenced by the 24th of March. The nest consists of a few dry twigs, is always placed in a hole or under a projecting portion of the rock, seldom more than a foot from the surface, and never, as far as my experience goes, out of reach of the hand. On being caught, they make no noise, and do not resist at all, — unlike the Tropic Bird, which fights manfully, biting and screaming with all its might. The egg does not seem to me to resemble an ordinary hen's egg; the shell is much more fragile and more highly polished. I broke a number of them in endeavoring to remove the bird from the nest. They vary a good deal in size and form, some of them being quite rounded, and others elongated. Three of them measured as follows: one .059 by .036, another .052 by .033, and the third .051 by .037. Both sexes incubate.

"Why these birds and the Stormy Petrels never enter or leave their holes in the daytime is one of the mysteries of nature; both of them feeding and flying all day, are yet never seen in the vicinity of their breeding-places before dark. When anchored in the night-time near one of the keys, on which they breed, their mournful note can be heard at all hours of the night; during the day they may be seen feeding in large flocks, generally out of sight of land. They do not fly round much, but remain most of the time quiet upon the surface of the water. I did not see one on the banks, and never saw them dive or apparently catching any fish, though they are often in company with Boobies and different species of Terns, all of which are actively employed in fishing. About half-way from Andros to the Bank, I saw on the 26th of April a flock of Boobies, Sooty Terns, Noddies, Cabot's Tern, and the Dusky Petrel, that covered the surface of the water, or hovering over it for an extent of at least a square mile. Their number must have been enormous."

The inhabitants claim that this species has received its local name of "Pimblico" from its cry; but I cannot perceive any resemblance between that name and the mournful notes which it utters, and therefore believe it to have originated differently.

Fig. Aud. Bds. N. A., Vol. VII. pl. 458.

FAM. PODICIPIDÆ.

GREBES.

PODICEPS DOMINICUS. (*Linn*)

ST. DOMINGO GREBE.

Winter Plumage, Male. — Above, dark brown, with slight greenish reflections; sides of the head and throat, ashy gray, continuous in a broad band around the neck; under parts, silky white, mottled with dusky; outer primaries showing chocolate-brown, the others and secondaries white.

Length 9.35, wing 3.60, tarsus 1.24, bill .85.

The pretty little St. Domingo Grebe is a resident, and not uncommon on some of the islands. It was quite abundant on Andros Island, and I was enabled to procure a number of specimens. It appears to prefer the pools in the dark recesses of the mangrove swamps to the more open ponds, and probably for this reason escaped the notice of previous collectors. Its habits apparently do not differ from other species of its family.

Gosse found this species breeding in Jamaica. He says, " Early in August I found near the edge of Mount Edgecombe Pond a nest of this Grebe,—a round heap of pond-weed and rotten leaves, flattened at the top and slightly hollowed. It was about fifteen inches wide, and six or eight thick. The top was damp, but not wet, and very warm from exposure to the sun's rays. We drew it on shore — for it was entangled among the branches of a fallen tree, but not attached to them — and presently found on the matted weed just below the surface, in the place where we had dragged it, a large white egg, excessively begrimed with dirt, doubtless from lying on the decayed leaves. On being cleansed, I found it covered with a chalky coat, easily scratched off. A few weeks after, I again visited this pond. On approaching before sunrise (for I had travelled by the brilliant starlight of the tropical heavens) I saw a Grebe sitting on a new nest in the same spot as I had found the former one. This nest was composed of similar materials, and contained four eggs. Early in December we found another nest, with young just peeping from the egg. It is probable, therefore, that several broods are reared in a season."

It probably breeds in the Bahamas, but we were unable to find its nest.

DISTRIBUTION OF SPECIES.

A GENERAL CATALOGUE OF THE BIRDS OF THE BAHAMA ISLANDS, SHOWING THOSE FOUND IN THE UNITED STATES, AND GIVING THE ISLANDS TO WHICH SOME SPECIES APPEAR TO BE RESTRICTED.

	Birds of the Bahamas.	Andros.	New Providence.	Abaco.	Inagua.	Bahamas (in general).	United States.
1.	Mimocichla plumbea . .		×	×			
2.	Mimocichla rubripes . .		×			×?	
3.	Margarops fuscatus				×		
4.	Mimus orpheus var. dominicus				×		
5.	Mimus bahamensis					×	
6.	Mimus carolinensis.					×	×
7.	Polioptila cærulea .					×	×
8.	Mniotilta varia					×	×
9.	Parula americana					×	×
10.	Helmitherus vermivorus					×	×
11.	Dendrœca æstiva					×	×
12.	Dendrœca petechia					×	
13.	Dendrœca petechia var. gaudlachi . .					×	.
14.	Dendrœca cærulescens					×	×
15.	Dendrœca coronata					×	×
16.	Dendrœca blackburniæ					×	×
17.	Dendrœca striata					×	×

Birds of the Bahamas.	Andros.	New Providence.	Abaco.	Inagua.	Bahamas (in general)	United States.
18. Dendrœca pennsylvanica					×	×
19. Dendrœca maculosa					×	×
20. Dendrœca tigrina					×	×
21. Dendrœca discolor					×	×
22. Dendrœca dominica					×	×
23. Dendrœca kirtlandi					×	×
24. Dendrœca palmarum					×	×
25. Dendrœca pinus					×	×
26. Siurus aurocapillus					×	×
27. Siurus noveboracensis					×	×
28. Geothlypis trichas					×	×
29. Geothlypis rostratus				×		
30. Setophaga ruticilla					×	×
31. Certhiola bahamensis					×	×?
32. Hirundo horreorum					×	×
33. Tachycineta bicolor					×?	×
34. Hirundo cyaneoviridis		×	×	×		
35. Vireo altiloquus var. barbatulus					×	×
36. Vireo flavifrons					×	×
37. Lanivireo crassirostris					×	
38. Loxigilla violacea					×	
39. Loxigilla noctis				×		
40. Passerculus savanna					×	×
41. Passer domesticus			×			

BIRDS OF THE BAHAMA ISLANDS.

Birds of the Bahamas.	Andros.	New Providence.	Abaco.	Inagua.	Bahamas (in general).	United States.
42. Cyanospiza ciris					×	×
43. Cyanospiza cyanea					×	×
44. Phonipara bicolor					×	×
45. Spindalis zena					×	(?)
46. Dolichonyx oryzivorus					×	×
47. Agelæus phœniceus					×	×
48. Tyrannus magnirostris				×		
49. Tyrannus caudafasciatus			×?			
50. Tyrannus griseus					×	
51. Myiarchus stolidus var. lucaysiensis					×	
52. Contopus bahamensis					×	
53. Pitangus bahamensis					×	
54. Antrostomus carolinensis					×	×
55. Chordeiles minor					×	
56. Doricha evelynæ					×	
57. Doricha lyrura				×		
58. Sporadinus recordi	×					
59. Sporadinus bracei			×			
60. Ceryle alcyon					×	×
61. Saurothera bahamensis		×			×?	
62. Coccyzus americanus					×	×
63. Coccyzus minor					×	×
64. Crotophaga ani					×	×
65. Picus villosus					×	×

Birds of the Bahamas.	Andros.	New Providence	Abaco.	Inagua.	Bahamas (in general).	United States.
66. Sphyrapicus varius .					×	×
67. Chrysotis collaria				×?	×	
68. Strix flammea var. pratincola .					×	
69. Speotyto cunicularia var. floridana					×	×
70. Circus hudsonicus . .					×	×
71. Accipiter fuscus .					×	×
72. Falco communis					×	×
73. Falco sparverius					×	×
74. Buteo borealis					×	×
75. Pandion haliætus . .					×	×
76. Cathartes aura	×		×			×
77. Columba leucocephala					×	×
78. Zenæda amabilis					×	×
79. Chamæpelcia passerina .					×	×
80. Geotrygon martinica . .					×	×
81. Ortyx virginianus					×	×
82. Squatarola helvetica . . .					×	×
83. Charadrius fulvus var. virginicus .					×	×
84. Ægialitis vociferus					×	×
85. Ægialitis wilsonius					×	×
86. Ægialitis semipalmatus					×	×
87. Ægialitis melodus .					×	×
88. Hæmatopus palliatus .					×	×
89. Strepsilas interpres					×	×

BIRDS OF THE BAHAMA ISLANDS.

BIRDS OF THE BAHAMAS.	Andros.	New Providence.	Abaco.	Inagua.	Bahamas (in general).	United States.
90. Himantopus nigricollis					X	X
91. Gallinago wilsoni					X	X
92. Macrorhamphus griseus					X	X
93. Ereunetes pusillus					X	X
94. Tringa minutilla					X	X
95. Tringa maculata					X	X
96. Tringa bonapartei					X	X
97. Calidris arenaria					X	X
98. Totanus semipalmatus					X	X
99. Totanus melanoleucus					X	X
100. Totanus flavipes					X	X
101. Tringoides macularius					X	X
102. Platalea ajaja					X	X
103. Ardea herodias					X	X
104. Ardea egretta					X	X
105. Ardea candidissima					X	X
106. Ardea leucogastra var. leucoprymna					X	X
107. Ardea cyanirostris				X		
108. Ardea rufa					X	X
109. Ardea cærulea					X	X
110. Ardea virescens					X	X
111. Nyctiardea violacea					X	X
112. Ardetta exilis					X	X
113. Rallus longirostris					X	X

Birds of the Bahamas.	Andros.	New Providence	Abaco.	Inagua.	Bahamas (in general).	United States.
114. Porzana carolina					×	×
115. Gallinula galeata					×	×
116. Porphyrio martinica					×	×
117. Fulica americana					×	×
118. Phœnicopterus rubra					×	×
119. Anser hiberboreus					×	×
120. Dendrocygna arborea					×	
121. Anas boschas					×	×
122. Dafila bahamensis					×	
123. Querquedula discors					×	×
124. Querquedula carolinensis					×	×
125. Fuligula affinis					×	×
126. Fuligula collaris					×	×
127. Fuligula ferina					×	×
128. Eresmatura rubida					×	×
129. Sula fiber					×	×
130. Sula dactylatra					×?	
131. Pelecanus fuscus					×	×
132. Graculus dilophus var. floridanus					×	×
133. Tachypetes aquilus					×	×
134. Phaethon flavirostris					×	×
135. Larus atricilla					×	×
136. Larus philadelphia					×	×
137. Sterna anglica					×	×

BIRDS OF THE BAHAMA ISLANDS. 231

BIRDS OF THE BAHAMAS.	Andros.	New Providence.	Abaco.	Inagua.	Bahamas (in general).	United States.
138. Sterna regia.					×	×
139. Sterna cantiaca					×	×
140. Sterna hirundo					×	×
141. Sterna paradisæa					×	×
142. Sterna supercillaris					×	×
143. Sterna fuliginosa					×	×
144. Sterna anosthæta					×	×
145. Anous stolidus					×	×
146. Oceanites oceanica					×	×
147. Puffinus major					×	×
148. Puffinus obscurus					×	×
149. Podiceps dominicus					×	×

APPENDIX.

APPENDIX.

A LIST OF BIRDS *NOT RECORDED* FROM THE BAHAMA ISLANDS, BUT WHICH MIGHT OCCASIONALLY OCCUR THERE, WITH NOTES GIVING THE PRINCIPAL CHARACTERISTICS BY WHICH THEY MAY BE IDENTIFIED.

1. *Turdus migratorius.* ROBIN. — Head and tail, blackish; under parts, reddish brown; throat marked with white and black. Length about 9.50, wing about 5.

2. *Turdus mustelinus.* WOOD THRUSH. — Below, white; breast and throat spotted on the sides; legs, pinkish. Length about 7.25, wing about 4.

3. *Turdus pallasii.* HERMIT THRUSH. — Below, white; breast and throat mottled on the sides; legs, yellowish. Length about 7, wing 3.25.

4. *Turdus swainsoni.* OLIVE-BACKED THRUSH. — Breast and throat thickly marked with spots of olive. Length about 7, wing about 4.

5. *Turdus fuscescens.* WILSON'S THRUSH. — Under parts, white; olive on the sides, sides of breast and throat, with small, fine spots. Length about 7, wing about 4.

6. *Mimus polyglottus.* MOCKING-BIRD.—Wings with two white bars; under parts, ashy and white. Length 9.50, wing 4.10.

7. *Buteo pennsylvanicus.* BROAD-WINGED BUZZARD. — Wing short and broad; a dark maxillary patch. Length about 17, wing about 10.

8. *Cathartes atratus.* BLACK VULTURE. — General plumage, black, feathers reaching the skull. Length about 24, wing about 17.

9. *Macropalama himantopus.* STILT SANDPIPER. — *Winter.* Above, gray; under parts, white. Length about 8, wing about 5. Easily recognized by its long legs.

10. *Limosa fedoa.* GREAT-MARBLED GODWIT. — Bill, pinkish, tipped with black; general plumage, pale reddish-brown; mottled. Length about 17, wing about 9.

11. *Totanus chloropus.* GREEN SHANKS.— Resembles *T. flavipes.* Legs, greenish; rump and tail, white, sometimes slightly mottled. Length about 12, wing about 6.50.

12. *Totanus solitarius.* SOLITARY TATTLER. — Bill, straight; legs, dark olive-brown, speckled with gray; under parts, white. Length about 8, wing about 5.

13. *Numenius longirostris.* LONG-BILLED CURLEW. — Bill very long, curved, often measuring over eight inches; plumage, brownish; legs, dark. Length about 23, wing about 11.

APPENDIX. 237

14. *Numenius hudsonicus.* HUDSONIAN CURLEW. — Resembles the last. Bill about 3.75.

15. *Tantalus loculator.* WOOD IBIS. — Adult, head and neck bare (young, feathered whitish); plumage, white; some of primaries purplish black; bill very long and stout. Length about 50, wing about 20.

16. *Ibis falcinellus var. ordii.* GLOSSY IBIS. — Plumage, chestnut and greenish. Length about 24, wing about 10.

17. *Ibis alba.* WHITE IBIS. — About size of the last; plumage white, outer primaries tipped with black; young, brownish gray.

18. *Ibis rubra.* SCARLET IBIS. — About size of the last; plumage, bright scarlet, outer primaries tipped with black; young, gray, sometimes mottled with scarlet.

19. *Botaurus minor.* BITTERN. — General plumage, brownish, streaked with tawny and black; legs, greenish; soles of the feet, yellow. Length about 25, wing about 10.

20. *Nyctiardea grisea var. nævia.* NIGHT HERON. — Bill more slender than that of *N. violacea*, resembling that species; head only slightly crested. Length about 23, wing about 12.

21. *Rallus virginianus.* VIRGINIA RAIL. — Resembles *R. longirostris;* small. Length about 9, wing about 4.

APPENDIX.

22. *Porzana jamaicensis.* BLACK RAIL.— Plumage dark; head and under parts, dark slate; primaries with small white spots. Length about 5.25, wing 2.75.

23. *Anas obscura.* DUSKY DUCK. — Plumage, mottled dark brown, patch of dark blue on the wings. Length about 23, wing about 10.

24. *Dafila acuta.* PINTAIL. — Central tail-feathers much prolonged; under parts, white. Length about 24, wing about 11.

25. *Spatula clypeata.* SHOVELLER DUCK.— Bill very broad at the end; head and neck of the male, green; belly, chestnut. Length about 20, wing about 10.

26. *Aix sponsa.* WOOD DUCK. — Head, with crest, marked with green, chestnut, and black; breast, chestnut, speckled with white. A beautiful species.

27. *Bucephala clangula.* GOLDEN-EYED DUCK.— Head and part of neck, green; white spot on the check near the base of the bill. Length about 17, wing about 8.

28. *Bucephala albeola.* BUFFLE-HEADED DUCK. — A kind of crest; head, green, white, and purple; breast and under parts, white. Length about 15, wing about 6.

29. *Pelecanus trachyrhynchus.* WHITE PELICAN. — General plumage, white; sac, yellow. Length about 65.

30. *Larus argentatus.* HERRING GULL. — Above, pearl-gray; below, white; bill, yellow, showing a red spot; feet, flesh-color. Length about 25, wing about 16.

31. *Larus delawarensis.* RING-BILLED GULL. — Bill, dull yellow, with black band near the tip. Length about 18, wing about 14.

32. *Sterna galericulata.* ELEGANT TERN. — Bill, bright red, paling at the tip; legs and feet, black; crown and crest, black; *under parts showing rose color.* Length about 18.50, wing about 12.25.

33. *Sterna trudeaui.* TRUDEAU'S TERN. — Bill, orange, marked with black; entire plumage, grayish; a band through the eye. Length about 12, wing about 9.50.

34. *Sterna forsteri.* FOSTER'S TERN. — No black cap; under parts, white; a black band through the eye; bill dark. Length about 12.50, wing about 10.

35. *Rhynchops nigra.* BLACK SHIMMER. — Above, black; under parts, white; bill, red and black; the under mandible much longer than the upper; very thin. Length about 18, wing about 14.

36. *Podilymbus podiceps.* PIED-BILLED GREBE. — Bill with black bar; black patch on the throat; upper parts dark; under parts, white, sometimes marked with dusky. Length about 13, wing about 5.

INDEX.

INDEX.

A.

	PAGE
Accipiter fuscus,	128
Ægialitis melodus,	148
Ægialitis semipalmatus,	148
Ægialitis vociferus,	145
Ægialitis wilsonius,	147
Agelæus phœniceus,	98
Anas boschas,	184
Ani,	118
Anous stolidus,	216
Anser hyperboreus,	182
Antrostomus carolinensis,	104
Ardea candidissima,	167
Ardea cærulea,	171
Ardea cyanirostris,	168
Ardea egretta,	167
Ardea herodias,	166
Ardea leucogastra var. leucoprymna,	168
Ardea rufa,	170
Ardea virescens,	171
Ardetta exilis,	174
Arsnicker,	166

B.

	PAGE
Bahama Cuckoo,	116
Bahama Duck,	185
Bahama Finch,	92
Bahama Honey Creeper,	76

	PAGE
Bahama Kingbird,	102
Bahama Mocking-bird,	48
Bahama Swallow,	79
Bahama Woodstar,	108
Barn Owl,	125
Barn Swallow,	78
Belted Kingfisher,	115
Bittern, Least,	174
Black and White Creeper,	54
Black Charles,	87
Black and Yellow Warbler,	62
Black Grosbeak,	87
Black-bellied Plover,	144
Black-faced Finch,	91
Black-headed Gull (Laughing),	208
Black-poll Warbler,	61
Black-throated Blue Warbler,	58
Black-whiskered Vireo,	82
Blackbird, Red-winged,	98
Blackburnian Warbler,	60
Blue-gray Gnatcatcher,	52
Blue-winged Teal,	186
Blue Yellow-backed Warbler,	55
Bobolink,	97
Booby Gannet,	91
Bonaparte's Gull,	209
Brace's Humming-bird,	113
Bridled Tern,	215

INDEX.

	PAGE		PAGE
Brown Pelican,	196	Cyanospiza ciris,	89
Bull Peep (Sanderling),	160	Cyanospiza cyanea,	90
Buteo borealis,	131		
Buzzard,	134	D.	
C.		Dafila bahamensis,	185
Calidris arenaria,	160	Death Bird,	104
Cape May Warbler,	63	Dendrocygna arborea,	183
Carolina Rail,	176	Dendrœca æstiva,	56
Catbird,	51	Dendrœca blackburniæ,	60
Cathartes aura,	134	Dendrœca cærulescens,	58
Certhiola bahamensis,	76	Dendrœca coronata,	59
Ceryle alcyon,	115	Dendrœca discolor,	64
Chamæpelia passerina,	139	Dendrœca dominica,	65
Charadrius fulvus var. virginicus,	145	Dendrœca kirtlandi,	66
Chestnut-sided Warbler,	62	Dendrœca maculosa,	62
Chordeiles minor,	106	Dendrœca palmarum,	68
Chrysotis collaria,	123	Dendrœca pennsylvanica,	62
Chuck-wills-widow,	104	Dendrœca petechia,	57
Circus cyaneus var. hudsonius,	128	Dendrœca petechia var. gundlachi,	58
Clapper Rail,	176	Dendrœca pinus	69
Coccyzus americanus,	117	Dendrœca striata,	61
Coccyzus minor,	117	Dendrœca tigrina,	63
Columba leucocephala,	137	Dolichonyx oryzivorus,	97
Common Tern,	211	Doricha evelynæ,	108
Common Vireo,	83	Doricha lyrura,	110
Contopus bahamensis,	101	Dove, Ground,	139
Coot,	178	Dove, Key West,	141
Cormorant, Florida,	198	Dove, Zenaida,	138
Creeper, Bahama Honey,	76	Duck, Bahama,	185
Creeper, Black and White,	54	Duck, Lesser Black-headed,	187
Crotophaga ani,	118	Duck, Red-headed,	189
Crow,	134	Duck, Ring-necked,	188
Cuckoo, Bahama,	116	Duck, Ruddy,	189
Cuckoo, Mangrove,	117	Duck, Tree,	183
Cuckoo, Yellow-billed,	117	Dusky Shearwater,	219

INDEX

E.

	PAGE
Egg Bird,	204
Egret, Great White,	167
Egret, Little White,	167
Egret, Reddish,	170
English Sparrow,	88
Ereunetes pusillus,	157
Erismatura rubida,	189

F.

Falco communis,	129
Falco sparverius,	130
Falcon, Peregrine,	129
Falcon Sparrow,	130
Fighter,	102
Finch, Bahama,	92
Finch, Black-faced,	91
Fish Hawk,	131
Flamingo,	180
Florida Burrowing Owl,	126
Florida Cormorant,	198
Florida Gallinule,	177
Flycatcher, Gray,	99
Flycatcher, Great-billed,	99
Flycatcher, Least Bahama,	101
Flycatcher, Rufous-tailed,	100
Frigate.	200
Fulica americana,	178
Fuligula affinis,	187
Fuligula collaris,	188
Fuligula ferina var. americana,	189

G.

Gallinago wilsoni,	156
Gallinula galeata,	177

	PAGE
Gallinule, Florida,	177
Gallinule, Purple,	178
Gannet, Booby,	191
Geothlypis rostratus,	73
Geothlypis trichas.	72
Geotrygon martinica,	141
Gnat-catcher, Blue-gray,	52
Goatsucker,	104
Golden-crowned Thrush,	70
Golden Plover,	145
Gollden,	173
Goose, Snow,	182
Graculus dilophus var. floridanus,	198
Gray Flycatcher,	99
Great-billed Flycatcher,	99
Great Blue Heron,	166
Great White Egret,	167
Greater Shearwater,	218
Greater Yellow-leg,	161
Greater Yellow-throated Warbler,	73
Grebe, St. Domingo,	222
Green Heron,	171
Green-winged Teal,	187
Grosbeak, Black,	87
Grosbeak, Purple,	85
Ground Dove,	139
Gull, Bonaparte's,	209
Gull, Laughing,	208
Gull-billed Tern,	209
Gundlach's Warbler,	58

H.

Hæmatopus palliatus,	150
Hairy Woodpecker,	120
Hawk, Marsh,	128

INDEX.

	PAGE		PAGE
Hawk, Red-tailed,	131	Larus philadelphia,	209
Hawk, Sharp-shinned,	128	Laughing Gull,	208
Helmitherus vermivorus,	56	Least Bahama Flycatcher,	101
Heron, Great Blue,	166	Least Bittern,	174
Heron, Green,	171	Least Sandpiper,	158
Heron, Inagua,	168	Least Tern,	213
Heron, Little Blue,	171	Lesser Black-headed Duck,	187
Heron, Louisiana,	168	Little Blue Heron,	171
Heron, Yellow-crowned Night,	173	Little Mocking-bird,	48
Himantopus nigricollis,	153	Little Night Hawk,	106
Hirundo cyaneoviridis,	79	Little White Egret,	167
Hirundo horreorum,	78	Louisiana Heron,	168
Humming-bird, Bahama,	108	Loxigilla noctis,	87
Humming-bird, Brace's,	113	Loxigilla violacea,	85
Humming-bird, Lyre-tailed,	110	Lyre-tailed Humming-bird,	110
Humming-bird, Riccord's,	111		

I.

Inagua Heron,	168		
Indigo Bird,	90		

M.

Macrorhamphus griseus,	157
Mallard,	184
Mangrove Cuckoo,	117
Man-of-war Bird,	200

K.

Key West Dove,	141	Margarops fuscatus,	47
Kildeer Plover,	145	Marsh Hawk,	128
Kingbird, Bahama,	102	Maryland Yellow-throated Warbler,	72
Kingfisher, Belted,	115	Mimocichla plumbea,	45
Kirtland's Warbler,	66	Mimocichla rubripes,	46
		Mimus bahamensis,	48
		Mimus carolinensis,	51
		Mimus orpheus var. dominicus,	48

L.

		Mniotilta varia,	54
		Mocking-bird, Bahama,	48
Lanivireo crassirostris,	83	Mocking-bird, Little,	48
Larus atricilla,	208	Myiarchus stolidus var. leucaysiensis,	100

N.

	PAGE
Night Hawk, Little,	106
Night Heron,	173
Noddy Tern,	216
Nonpareil,	89
Nyctiardea violacea,	173

O.

Oceanites oceanica,	218
Ortyx virginianus,	142
Osprey,	131
Owl, Barn,	125
Owl, Florida Burrowing,	126
Oyster Catcher,	150

P.

Pandion haliætus,	131
Parrot,	123
Parrot Duck (local),	186
Passerculus savanna,	88
Passer domesticus,	88
Partridge,	141
Parula americana,	55
Paw-paw Bird,	47
Paw-paw Thrush,	47
Pectoral Sandpiper,	159
Peeps (Scolopacidæ),	156
Pelican, Brown,	196
Pelicanus fuscus,	196
Peregrine Falcon,	129
Petrel, Wilson's,	218
Phaethon flavirostris,	204
Phœnicopterus ruber,	180

	PAGE
Phonipara bicolor,	91
Picus villosus,	120
Pigeon, White-headed,	137
Pine Creeping Warbler,	69
Piping Plover,	148
Pitangus bahamensis,	102
Platalea ajaja,	164
Plover, Black-bellied,	144
Plover, Golden,	145
Plover, Kildeer,	145
Plover, Piping,	148
Plover, Ring-necked,	148
Plover, Wilson's.	147
Plumbeous Thrush,	45
Podiceps dominicus,	222
Polioptila cærulea,	52
Porphyris martinica,	178
Porzana carolina,	176
Prairie Warbler,	64
Puffinus major,	218
Puffinus obscurus,	219
Purple Gallinule,	178
Purple Grosbeak,	85

Q.

Quail,	141
Querquedula carolinensis,	187
Querquedula discors,	186

R.

Rail, Carolina,	176
Rail, Clapper,	176
Rallus longirostris,	176

INDEX.

	PAGE
Rain Crow,	118
Red-Breasted Snipe,	157
Reddish Egret,	170
Red-headed Duck,	189
Red-legged Thrush,	46
Redstart,	75
Red-tailed Hawk,	131
Red-winged Blackbird,	98
Riccord's Humming-bird,	111
Ring-necked Duck,	188
Ring-necked Plover,	148
Roseate Tern,	212
Royal Tern,	210
Ruddy Duck,	189
Rufous-tailed Flycatcher,	100

S.

	PAGE
Sanderling,	160
Sandpiper, Least,	158
Sandpiper, Pectoral,	159
Sandpiper, Sanderling,	160
Sandpiper, Semipalmated,	157
Sandpiper, Spotted,	162
Sandpiper, White rumpled,	159
Sandwich Tern,	211
Saurothera bahamensis,	116
Savanna Sparrow,	88
Sea Pie,	150
Sea Swallow (Tern),	211
Sciurus aurocapillus,	70
Sciurus noreboracensis,	71
Semipalmated Sandpiper,	157
Setophaga ruticilla,	75
Sharp-shinned Hawk,	128

	PAGE
Shearwater, Dusky,	219
Shearwater, Greater,	218
Snipe, Red-breasted,	157
Snipe, Wilson's,	156
Snow Goose,	182
Sooty Tern,	214
Spanish Paroquet,	85
Sparrow, English,	88
Sparrow, Falcon,	130
Sparrow, Savanna,	88
Spheotyto cunicularia var. floridana,	126
Sphyrapicus varius,	121
Spindalis zena,	92
Spoonbill,	164
Sporadinus bracei,	113
Sporadinus ricordi,	111
Spotted Sandpiper,	162
Squatarola helvetica,	144
St. Domingo Grebe,	222
Sterna anglica,	209
Sterna anosthæta,	215
Sterna cantiaca,	211
Sterna fuliginosa,	214
Sterna hirundo,	211
Sterna paradisæa,	212
Sterna regia,	210
Sterna superciliaris,	213
Stilt,	153
Strepsilas interpres,	151
Strix flammea var. pratincola,	125
Sula dactylatra,	194
Sula fiber,	191
Summer Warbler,	56
Swallow, Bahama,	79
Swallow, Barn,	78
Swallow, White-bellied,	80

T.

	PAGE
Tachycineta bicolor,	80
Tachypetes aquilus,	200
Teal, Blue-winged	186
Teal, Green-winged,	187
Tern, Bridled,	215
Tern, Common,	211
Tern, Gull-billed,	209
Tern, Least,	213
Tern, Noddy,	216
Tern, Roseate,	212
Tern, Royal,	210
Tern, Sandwich,	211
Tern, Sooty,	214
Thrush, Golden-crowned,	70
Thrush, Paw-paw,	47
Thrush, Plumbeous,	45
Thrush, Red-legged,	46
Thrush, Water,	71
Tobacco Dove,	139
Totanus flavipes,	162
Totanus melanoleucus,	161
Totanus semipalmatus,	160
Tree Duck,	183
Tringa bonapartei,	159
Tringa maculata,	159
Tringa minutilla,	158
Tringoides macularius,	162
Tropic Bird,	204
Turkey Buzzard,	134
Turnstone,	151
Tyrannus caudifasciatus,	99
Tyrannus griseus,	99
Tyrannus magnirostris,	99

V.

	PAGE
Vireo altiloquus var. barbatulus,	82
Vireo, Black-whiskered,	82
Vireo, Common,	83
Vireo flavifrons,	83
Vireo, Yellow-throated,	83

W.

Warbler, Black and Yellow,	6
Warbler, Blackburnian,	60
Warbler, Black-poll,	61
Warbler, Black-throated Blue,	58
Warbler, Blue Yellow-backed,	55
Warbler, Cape May,	63
Warbler, Chestnut-sided,	62
Warbler, Greater Yellow-throated,	73
Warbler, Gundlach's,	58
Warbler, Kirtland's,	66
Warbler, Maryland Yellow-throated,	72
Warbler, Pine-creeping,	69
Warbler, Prairie,	64
Warbler, Summer,	56
Warbler, Worm-eating,	56
Warbler, Yellow Red-poll,	68
Warbler, Yellow-rumpled,	69
Warbler, Yellow-throated,	65
Water Thrush,	71
Whistling Duck,	183
White-bellied Swallow,	80
White-headed Pigeon,	137
White-rumpled Sandpiper,	159
Willet,	161
Wilson's Petrel,	218

	PAGE		PAGE
Wilson's Plover,	147	Yellow-crowned Night Heron.	173
Wilson's Snipe,	156	Yellow-leg,	162
Wood Dove,	138	Yellow-leg, Greater,	161
Woodpecker, Hairy,	120	Yellow Red-poll Warbler,	68
Woodpecker, Yellow-bellied,	121	Yellow-rumpled Warbler,	59
Woodstar, Bahama,	106	Yellow-throated Vireo,	83
Worm-eating Warbler,	56	Yellow-throated Warbler,	65

Y.

| Yellow-bellied Woodpecker, | 121 |
| Yellow-billed Cuckoo, | 117 |

Z.

| Zenaida amabilis, | 138 |
| Zenaida Dove, | 138 |